THE NEW ORLEANS FRENCH

NOUVELLE ORLEANS Capitale de la LOUISIANE.

Échelle de 900 Toises.

1 Place d'Arme
2 Église Paroissiale
3 Logement des Capucins Curés
4 Gouvernement
6 Intendance
6 Conseil
7·7 Casernes
8·8 Magazins
9·10 Corps de garde et Prison
11 Religieuses Ursulines et Hôpital
12 Poudrière
13 Levée.

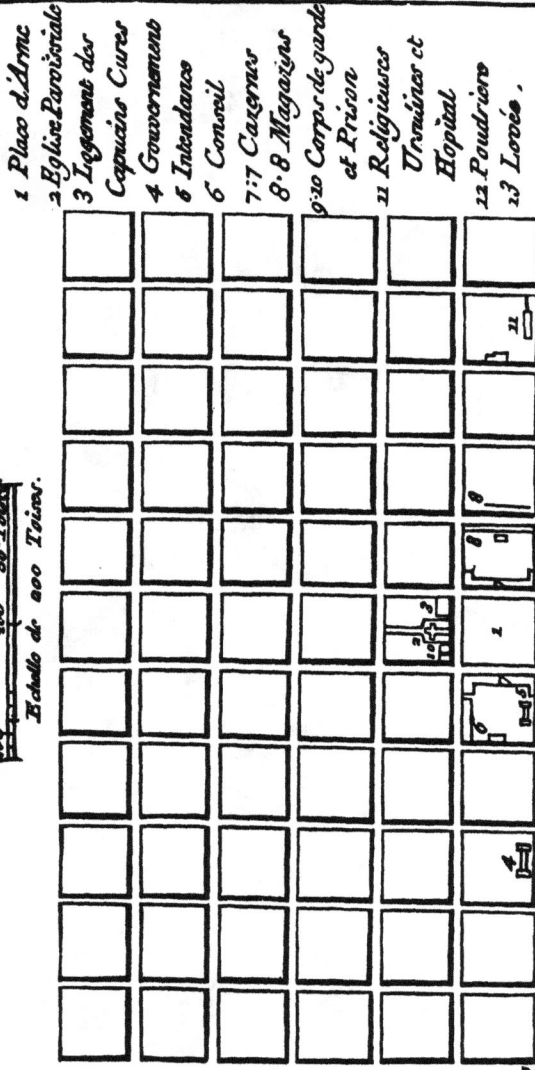

Fleuve S.t Louis.

An early French plan of New Orleans, showing its grid-iron lay-out

From: "History of America" edited by Justin Winsor, London, 1887

The
New Orleans French

1720-1733

A collection of marriage records
relating to the first colonists
of the Louisiana Province.

By
Winston De Ville

CLEARFIELD COMPANY

Library of Congress Card Number 75 - 150967
International Standard Book Number 0 - 8063 - 0480 - 4

Copyright © 1973
Genealogical Publishing Co., Inc.
Baltimore, Maryland
All rights reserved.

Reprinted for
Clearfield Company, Inc. by
Genealogical Publishing Co., Inc.
Baltimore, Maryland
1994

Made in the United States of America

CONTENTS

Frontispiece

PREFACE

When these documents were first recorded New Orleans was only two years old, but Mobile had already begun to prosper and settlers were populating the entire Gulf Coast. It is to most of these early settlers and those of the Mississippi Valley that these marriages relate. Researchers will also find references to the German Coast, Pointe Coupée, Natchitoches, and Yazoo Post in Mississippi and Illinois. Even "les Rapides," then in the hinterlands, is mentioned, while Biloxi and Mobile figure prominently in the documents. Of special distinction are the records after 1729, which hint at the dramatic story of the Natchez Massacre by listing many principals as widows and widowers of the Fort Rosalie tragedy.

This publication should be of considerable use to historians of the Mississippi Valley and to genealogists of the French Louisiana Province. It must be stressed here that these notes are the results of this editor's translations of a Spanish priest's transcripts made in the late 18th Century of records originally written by French missionary priests earlier in that century. The original registers were probably nearly illegible, so that proper spelling is now often impossible to determine. Experienced researchers will recognize the problem, beginners are advised to be cautious, and all are counseled to examine photocopies of the records in the vaults of the Basilica of St. Louis in New Orleans should any questions arise. These records are found in Marriage Book I and in "Baptismal" Book I. Any entry can be easily located by referring to the date.

The form this publication takes is self-explanatory: in alphabetical order the male is listed first in bold type, followed by the female, also in bold type. In most cases, parents, places of origin, former spouses, and other important data are given. An Addendum lists the priests as they appeared in the records and the Index will guide the researchers to unalphabetized patronymics.

Work on this book began in 1962 when research in ecclesiastical registers in Louisiana was almost unknown. Since then, and with the

THE NEW ORLEANS FRENCH

enlightened cooperation of such people as Basilica of St. Louis Archivist Gertrude Saucier and Msgr. Henry C. Bezou, who graciously helped me in securing access to the records in the first place, most of the Louisiana church records have been made available. For their help I am thankful. Others have encouraged this and similar projects: Ruth Warren, my colleague at Mobile Public Library from 1963 to 1964; Lucy Kinsella and my neighbors in the 800 Block of Orleans Street in the Vieux Carré where, for five wonderful years, I worked on this book. Mrs. Kinsella worked, laughed and cried with me, and I am grateful. I first met Lena de Grummond only a few minutes before my first lecture in genealogy and, as I did then, I have asked for and received her good counsel many times since; Katherine Bridges' standards of research and writing have always been goals for me and her friendship is cherished; Jody Carrigan, in more recent years, has shared her extensive professional knowledge with me, and together we have been able to solve most of the world's social ills. In the early years of my genealogical research, Gilbert and Elinor Fletcher, now of Virginia, opened their Garden District home to me and constructively influenced my academic principles. W. V. Garnier has been a firm supporter of my history projects for several years (his enthusiasm and encouragement helped to build a significant collection of Louisiana materials at Morehouse Public Library in Bastrop). John Francis McDermott, the dean of Mississippi Valley historians, has provided me with a great deal of guidance when I needed it and inspiration to publish more primary source material in our field. If the historiography of Louisiana continues to flourish, it will be because these people, and a few others, refused to see our colonial records neglected without a fight. And it *has* been a fight; but we are winning and it is a good feeling.

And, at last, thanks to Tom D. Hall, Jr., Rick Dreibelbis, L. D. Clepper, Jr., and Glen Lee Greene, Jr., friends who have learned to accept the eccentricities of a genealogist and publisher.

Winston De Ville

Baltimore, 1972

THE NEW ORLEANS FRENCH

THE NEW ORLEANS FRENCH

⚜

17 September 1731

NICOLAS ADAM—native of Orleans, son of Michel Adam and Françoise de l'Etang, parisioners of New Orleans and **MARIE MARGUERITE ROY**—native of Montreal in Canada, daughter of Louis Roy and Marie Catherine du Mas, also parisioners of New Orleans. Present was Marie Jeanne Mignon, wife of Louis Roy and step-mother of the bride.

19 June 1730

ALAIN ALIZEL—son of Didier Alizel and Marie Tournelle, native of Breste, bishopric of Leon and **TOINETTE SURENNE**—daughter of Jean Baptiste Surenne and Jeanne Berry, native of Paris, parish of St. Germain L'Auxerois, widow of Jean Viel called Carpentras, who died in Louisiana.

6 July 1722

GILBERT ALONIER—son of Antoine Alonier and Jeanne Durand, native of Boin, diocese of Lion, widower of Fleury Gardon and **ELIZA-BETH D'ERIE**—daughter of Joseph D'Erie and Elizabeth Troos(?), native of Alsace.

3

THE NEW ORLEANS FRENCH

6 February 1730

FRANCOIS ARNAULT—resident on the lower river, son of Jean Arnault and Marie Trudeau, native of Montreal, parish of St. Sulpice and **BARBE CLAUDE MASSY**—daughter of Mr. Jean Massy and Catherine Aufret, native of Tours in Touraine, parish of St. Clement.

20 February 1722, Natchez

THOMAS ASSELIN—habitant of Yasous, son of Jean Asselin and Marguerite Grantelle and **JEANNETOZ**—daughter of Jean Hubert and [Blank].

18 April 1720, Mobile

NOEL AUBERT and **MARGUERITE ROCH**—native of Paris, parish of St. Eustache. [This record is a certification made on 12 May 1733.]

10 May 1728

PIERRE AUBUCHON—resident of the Parish of Kaskaskia, native of Montreal, son of Joseph Aubuchon and Elizabeth Cusson and **MARIE BRUNET**—native of Kaskaskia, daughter of Jean Brunet dit Bourbonnais and Elizabeth Deshaye, residents of Kaskaskia.

10 March 1723

JOSEPH AUGIBOT—native of Normotier in Poitou, son of Mathurin Augibot and Catherine [Blank] and **FRANCOIS BOIS**—native of La Rochelle, widow of Pierre Aubert.

4

THE NEW ORLEANS FRENCH

14 January 1732

RENE BABIN called La Flame—soldier in the company of Mr. de Gauvry, son of René Babin and Francoise Brian, native of La Madeleine of the town of Segret in Anjou, heretofore married to Therese Samuran, who died in Louisiana and **RENOTTE SALAIN**—widow of Jacques Bernard, who died in Louisiana, daughter of Nicolas Salain and Perinne Terhaut, native of Hennebon, bishopric of Vannes in Brittany.

4 January 1724

JEAN BACHAIRE and **JEANNE GILBERT**—daughter of deceased René Gilbert and Marguerite Burelle.

16 May 1722

CLAUDE BAGNOIR—son of Pierre Bagnoir and Louise Du Buy and **ANNE NAUMOINES**—daughter of Francois Naumoins [possibly Nanmoins] and Catherine Barbier.

16 August 1723

JOSEPH BAILLET—son of Claude Baillet and Francoise Coriere and **BARBE ALBRECHT**—widow of Magnus Albrecht. Both are of this parish.

25 June 1721

VIVIEN BAILLY—son of Julien Bailly and [Blank] and **MARIE BOQUET**—daughter of Jean Boquet and Denise Charlemagne.

THE NEW ORLEANS FRENCH

17 June 1721

GILBERT BARE—son of Jean Baré and Marie [Blank] and MARIE JEANNE GODEFROY—daughter of Claude Godefroy and Marie Boulard.

November 1726

PAUL BARRE—native of Ste. Marie, parish of Montreal, bishopric of Quebec, resident of English Turn, son of Jacques Barré and Elizabeth Jette and MARIE JEANNE GIRARDY—daughter of Joseph Girardy and Marie Jeanne Henry, resident of Bayou St. Jean.

7 April 1723

ETIENNE BARRON—native of La Perriere in Champagne, diocese of ' Langres and MARIE MAGDELAINE BOURU—native of Montargy.

4 April 1725

NICHOLAS BAUCHE called Picard—of Abbeuil, soldier of the company of Mr. Renaud garrisoned at Yazoux, son of Nicolas Bauche and Marie Beaulieu, inhabitant of Abbeville, parish of St. Sepulchre, bishopric of Amien and CATHERINE AMORU (?) [possibly Amom] — daughter of François Amoru (?), carpenter, and Françoise Lagratte, inhabitant of Ennebon, bishopric of Cornuaille.

15 May 1730

NICOLAS BAUCHE called Picard—native of Ableville in Picardy, son of Nicolas Bauche and Marie Boiliot, widower of Catherine Aniot, who died in Louisiana and ANNE MARIE PEVIFUE (?)—daughter of Antoine P - - - - - - and Dame Therese Manuel, native of Bruxelles, widow of Jean Baptiste Breda, who died at the Tonika Village.

6

THE NEW ORLEANS FRENCH

1 February 1723, German Coast

PIERRE BAYER—native of Blanckenloch near Tourbach [or Tourlach] on the Rhine and **MARGUERITE PELLERINE**—widow of Jean George Sibalte.

16 April 1730

MICHEL BEAU—resident of Natchez, native of the canton of Berne, Switzerland, widower of Francoise Freson [Treson ?], who died at Natchez and **JEANNE LASSY**—native of Lyon, parish of St. Nizier, widow of Jean Depassé called Beausejour, who died at Natchez.

28 October 1730

CHARLES BEAUSERGENT—native of Angers, parish of St. Moriel, son of Charles Beausergent and Marie Lalandie and **MARIE LEDE** (??)— native of Dieklingen, daughter of Philippe Scoup and Anne Marthe, widow of Jean Louis de Pain, who died at Natchez.

11 September 1730

GRATIEN BEDIEF—native of Tours in Tourraine, parish of La Ville aux Dames, son of Pierre Bedief and Marie, whose last name is not known and **LUCIE CRETZ**—native of Neufchatel in Switzerland, daughter of Joan Cretz and Jeanne Cranne, widow of Gabriel Morissiaux [or Monissiaux], who died at Natchez.

19 May 1721

LOUIS BEGNON—son of Francois Begnon and Mathurine Guinarde and **ELIZABETH DE LAUNAY**—daughter of Marau De Launay and Marie Baude [or Bauve].

THE NEW ORLEANS FRENCH

2 June 1722

PIERRE BEL—son of Pierre Bel and Marie Forte, widower of Isidore Thomassin, native of La Rochelle and **LOUISE FONTENELLE**—daughter of Jean Fontenelle and Francois Dubois, native of Rhounan.

4 April 1725

JEAN BAPTISTE BERGERON—inhabitant of the upper river, son of Leonard Bergeron and Marguerite Beauvais and **MARIE JEANNE DAUPHIN**—daughter of Joseph Dauphin, captain of arms in the department of Breste, and Elizabeth Perin Bourgeous of Breste.

5 February 1725

SIMON BERLINGER—native of Blanbeirein, in the duchy of Witenberg, habitant of this parish and **CATHERINE RODE**—widow of Jacob Herkorn, who died at L'Orient, and Joseph Muler, who died in this parish.

12 January 1728

SIMON BERLINGER—native of Blanberen, duchy of Witemberg, son of Luprerche (?) Berlinger and Barbe Fitzé [or Sitzé], widower of Cristine Kentzeré, who died in Louisiana and **ELIZABETH FLICK**—daughter of Jean Jacques Flick and Anne Marie Krebs, native of Biel, Marquisat of Badere, widow in second marriage of Joseph Sigeler, who died at L'Orient, bishopric of Vannes. Both are residents of German Village.

22 June 1721

JACQUES BERNARD called St. Jacques—son of Jacques Bernard and Francoise Splonzin and **DENISE ALIO**—daughter of Jacques Alio and Jeanne Segure. [The bride signed "Denis Alihome."]

19 June 1730

JACQUES BERNARD—resident of Illinois, native of the bishopric of Nantes, son of Jacques Bernard and François Plonzard, widower of Lorine Eliaume, who died in Illinois and RENEE SALAHUN—native of the bishopric of Vannes, daughter of Nicolas Salahun and Perine Lorhaut.

7 May 1721

SAMUEL BERNARD called St. Cautin—son of Leon St. Cautin and Judith Baillard and MARIE GENEVIEVE GERNIER—daughter of Pierre Gernier and Marie Jeanne.

16 February 1727

Renunciation of the Calvinist religion by MARIE BERNARDIN, born in the Canton of Berne, 18 years old. [See Dauphin.]

10 January 1723

ANDRE BERTAUD—native of Clausaux (?) in Poitou, diocese of Luçon, son of Etienne Bertault and Marie Gibottel and MARIE POITTEVINE—widow of Pierre Coignon, while living, a carpenter residing in this town.

23 April 1721

LEONARD BILLERON—son of Pierre Billeron and Marie Forciee [or Forcue] and MARIE CLAIRE CATOIRE—daughter of Pierre Catoire and Anne Potin.

THE NEW ORLEANS FRENCH

25 November 1727

BARTHELEMY BIMMONT—native of Paris, parish of St. Paul, son of deceased Francois Bimmont, bourgeois of Paris, and Magdelaine Dan [Daniel ?] and **JEANNE FRANCOISE MARON**—native of Paris, parish of St. Sulpice, daughter of Pierre Maroy and deceased Marie Anne Legrand (?), widow of Pierre Richaume, who died in Louisiana.

7 June 1721

JULIEN BINARD—native of St. Main, diocese of St. Malo, son of Robert Bernard (*sic*) and Marguerite Burel and **MARIE ANGELIQUE DIMANCHE**—native of Paris, parish of St. Sulpice, daughter of François Dimanche and Jeanne Amiot.

18 April 1725

PIERRE BINARD—turner of Rochefort, son of Pierre Binard, during his lifetime guard-of-the-park at Rochefort and Marie Matery of Blois and **CATHERINE CONIDEQUE**—daughter of Henry Conideque, of the parish of Lian, bishopric of Cornuaille, and deceased Marie Prouette, inhabitant of the same place.

28 February 1729

LOUIS JOSEPH BISOTTON, Sieur de St. Martin—officer of the Marine, son of deceased Mr. Charles Bisotton, Councilor of the King, Commissioner-Inquisitor and Examiner at the Chalet de Paris, and Dame Gabriel Perthuis and **MARGUERITE LA CHAISE**—daughter of Mr. de la Chaise, Commissioner of the King, and Her First Councilor on the Superior Council, and Marguerite Cailly.

10

THE NEW ORLEANS FRENCH

24 September 1721

GUILLAUME BLANCVILAIN and **MARGUERITE CRESPEL**.

16 April 1721

ROBERT BLANQUET—son of Michel Blanquet and Marie Hosas and **MARIE CATHERINE ANGRAND**—daughter of Nicolas Angrand and Elizabeth Flar (?).

3 April 1731

LOUIS BLAR—native of St. Pierre De Saumure, bishopric of Anjou, son of René Blar and Marguerite Feret, widower of Anne La Roulle, who died at Rapides and **THERESE MARQUIAN**—native of St. Humiez, bishopric of Grenoble, daughter of Desmien Marquian and Dimanche Terra.

9 November 1733

LOUIS BLAR—native of St. Pierre de Saumure, bishopric of Anjou, son of René Blar and Marguerite Feret, widower of Therese Marquian, who died in Louisiana and **RENAUTTE GOURMY**—daughter of Nicolas Gourmy and Marie Anne, native of Cannes, bishopric of Vannes.

18 February 1725

LOUIS BLAS [probably **BLAR**]—native of Anjou, carpenter, habitant of Natchitoches and **ANNE LE BOULLE**—native of the parish of Orienteque, bishopric of Vanne in Brittany.

11

THE NEW ORLEANS FRENCH

23 April 1721

JACQUES BLOUIN—son of Jacques Blouin and Francois Seret [possibly Feret] and ELIZABETH GIRARD—daughter of Jean Girard and Catherine de la Coste.

21 August 1722

JACQUES BLOUIN called La Croix—son of Jacques Blouin and Francoise Seré, native of the parish of Ste. Croix in Angers, now a resident of Natchez and MARIE ANNE DAUDESSO—daughter of Erman Daudesso and Magdelaine Castelan, native of the parish of St. Severin of Paris.

17 December 1731

LOUIS BOISSIER—soldier in the company of Mr. De Gauvry, son of Louis Boissier and Catherine Alin, native of Rennes in Brittany and MARIE PERSONET—daughter of François Personet and Louise Carie, native of Auré, bishopric of Vannes.

21 April 1727

CHARLES BONSERGENT called Langevin—habitant of Cannes Bruslées, native of Angers and MARIE FOUCARDE—native of Chateauneuf in Province, diocese of Grace, widow of Henry Pelegrin who died at Cannes Bruslées.

20 February 1730

LAURENT BORDELON—employee of the Company of the Indies, native of Havre de Grace, parish of Notre Dame, son of Jean Baptiste Thomas Bordelon, Director of the General Treasury for Rations of the Marine in the Department of Rochefort, and Mlle. Henriette de Rochechouart and **ANNE FRANCOISE ROLAND**—native of Paris, parish of St. Germain Lauxerois (?), daughter of Jean Baptiste Rolan, bourgeois, and Jeanne Bonnet, widow of Nicolas Sarrazin, who was guardian of the storehouse of this colony.

2 February 1728

MICHEL BORDIER—native of Tours, parish of St. Vincent, baker in the service of the Company and **FRANCOISE TRIPONET**—native of Switzerland, bishopric of Bal, daughter of Pierre Priponet and Jeanne _____ , widow of Pierre Bruzuaire (?), who died at Biloxi.

16 January 1726

JEAN BOSSIER—habitant of Natchitoches, son of Jean Bossier, laborer, and Marguerite Beron Cartasagra, from the bishopric of Cahors [or probably, native of Cartasagra, bishopric of Cahors] and **MARGUERITE FOGLE**—native of Souabe, daughter of Michel Fogle, habitant of the German Coast and Barbe Grisgry [or Guigry].

8 December 1722

LOUIS JEAN BOT—native of Montauban, son of Nicolas Jean Bot and Marie Jeanne and **WIDOW MADRON DE CHANAU**—daughter of Claude Vollain and Francoise Damaseau.

THE NEW ORLEANS FRENCH

10 February 1728

CLAUDE BOTSON—native of the bishopric of Chalon sur Manne [Marne ?], son of deceased Claude Botson and Marguerite Pieron, master *taillendier* of the town and **MAGDELAINE CHENE**—native of La Rochelle, parish of Notre Dame, daughter of Jean Chene and Marguerite Erboine, widow of René Duchesne, who died in Louisiana.

22 June 1733

FRANCOIS BOUCHER, esquire, Sieur Monbrun—son of Jean Baptiste Boucher, esquire, Sieur Monbrun, and Françoise Charet, native of the parish of Ste. Famille de Boucherville in Canada and **GENEVIEVE MONIQUE RIVART**—daughter of deceased Antoine Rivart and deceased Marie Driard, native of Dauphin Island, a dependence of this diocese.

12 May 1729

PIERRE BOUCHER—of Kaskaskia, son of deceased Jean Boucher and Jeanne Roussaud, native of Perigueux, widower of Jeanne Roussaud (*sic*), who died in Illinois and **CATHERINE FENEROLLE**—daughter of François Fenerolle and Anne Marie le Saret, native of Sarlouis, diocese of Treve (?), widow of Jean Nadot, master carpenter, who died in Louisiana.

9 June 1721

JEAN BOURBEAU—son of Dominique Bourbeau and Marguerite Tabois [or Tabon] and **ELIZABETH LE FAURE** called Dumont—daughter of Pierre Le Faure and Catherine de Lordre.

14

21 February 1722, Natchez

FRANCOIS BOURDON—master carpenter, son of Francois Bourdon and Jacqueline Le Roy and **MARIE JEANNE GELAIN**—daughter of Francois Gelain and Joseph Lucas.

5 October 1726

FRANCOIS BOURDON—master carpenter, native of Montreuil, diocese of Amien, widow of deceased Marie Jeanne Jelin, who died in Louisiana and **MARIE KASNERAL**—native of Pleixan (?), archbishopric of Strasbourg, widow of Antoine Kichelruei (??), who died in Louisiana.

22 June 1721

NICOLAS CHARLES BOURGEOIS—son of Louis Alexander Bourgeois and Francoise Gratien and **ANNE LE VASSEUR**—daughter of Charles Vasseur and Nicole Caho.

30 October 1730

NICOLAS CHARLES BOURGEOIS—native of Paris, parish of St. Sulpice, widower of Anne Le Vasseur [possibly Le Vanneur], son of Louis Alexandre Bourgeois and Francoise Grattin and **MARIE JOSEPHE TARAU**—native of Grausin (?), bishopric of Cambray, daughter of Joseph Tarau and Thereze Delsine (?). One Jean Rondot signed as a witness.

10 June 1721

FRANCOIS BOUVET—son of Laurent Bouvet and Perine Laudeze and **MARIE LAMBAGOIS**—daughter of Jean Baptiste Lambagois and Marie Anne de France.

8 July 1721

FRANCOIS BRACHON—native of the parish of Darnecy in Savoye, son of Edmé Brachon and **JEANNE COURLIE**—native of the same place, daughter of Claude Bertrand Courlié and Francoise Richard.

30 November 1733

NICOLAS BRANTAN—native of Huningric in Alsace, diocese of Bale, son of Dominique Brantan and Marie Anne Hubler and **GABRIELLE MORAN**—native of Orange, daughter of Francois Moran, widow of Francois Raclot, who died in Louisiana.

16 August 1721

LOUIS BRET—widower of Elizabeth Rouet and **MARIE BAUDOUIN**—widow of Pierre Marioche.

24 August 1729

PIERRE BRIDEL—son of Barthelemy Bridel and Jeanne Masson, native of Vitré in Brittany, soldier in the Company of Dutisné and **ANNE MARGUERITE ZUICK** (?)—native of Bowwvler (?) in Alsace, daughter of Jean Adam Zwick (?) and Anne Koen.

29 October 1726

LOUIS BROUET—master wheelright, son of Robert Brouet, bourgeois of Paris, and Magdelaine Aguet [or Aquet], native of the parish of St. Paul, archbishopric of Paris, widow from the first marriage of Francoise Diran and **MARIE KRESMEIKA**—minor daughter of Bastien Kresmeika and Marguerite Walhee (?), native of the bishopric of Spire (?).

16

THE NEW ORLEANS FRENCH

26 September 1729

MR. IGNACE FRANCOIS BROUTIN—captain-engineer in this colony and commandant at Natchez, son of Pierre Broutin and Michel Lemairée [possibly Lemairet], native of the town of Bassée, bishopric of Arras and **MARIE MAGDELAINE LEMAIRE**—daughter of Pierre Lemaire and Marguerite Lamotte, native of Paris, parish of St. Sulpice, widow of Mr. de Mandeville, who was a major of New Orleans while living.

13 November 1731

FRANCOIS BRUNET—*taillendier*, native of Planiouet, parish of St. Sauveur, bishopric of St. Brieux, son of Fleuriant Brunet and Jeanne Brouazelle and **MARIE ELECQ**—native of Bibri, bishopric of Vasmes, daughter of Pierre Elecq and Marie Tandie, widow of Jean Belmer called St. Jean Patron (?), who died at Natchez.

11 September 1730

JEAN DENIS BUA—native of Tounon in Savoye, widower of Claudine Rochelle, who died at Cap Francois and **MARIE ANNE ANGRAND** [or Augrand]—native of Dair [or Dain—probably Hedin], in Artois, bishopric of St. Omer, widow of Ameline Foueau, who died at Natchez.

8 May 1728

NOEL HENRY BUISSON—Inspector of Indigo in Louisiana, native of Rhennes in Brittany, parish of St. Aubin, son of Louis Buisson and Francoise Le Roy and **MARIE ANNE BERTIN**—native of Rhouan in Normandy, parish of St. Vig—(?), daughter of Germain Bertin and Marie Marthe de Lamare.

22 February 1725

MICHEL CABASSIER—native of Montreal, bishopric of Quebec and MARIE THEREZE DUPRE—widow of Jean Joseph Martino.

7 May 1731

SIMON FRANCOIS CALAIS—voyager, native of Cotecambresy, archbishopric of Cambray, son of Bernard Calais and Marguerite Pezier and MARIE MARGUERITE MOULIE—native of Rochefort, bishopric of Chartres, daughter of Jean Moulié and Marguerite Autour (or Aubour), widow of Jacques Joseph Catherine called Capitaine, who died at Natchez.

16 June 1721

PIERRE CAMBRE—native of Mauberge and MARIE CATHERINE DE RENNE—native of Le Fontaine. Both parties are on the Concession of Mr. Adam.

16 April 1730

JACQUES CANTRELLE—native of St. Leger in Picardy, diocese of Amien, son of Claude Cantrelle and Marguerite Eurquin, widower of Marie Francoise Minquelze, who died at Natchez and MARIE MARGUERITE LARMUSIAU—native of Rhemmes in Henault, daughter of Jean Baptiste Larmusiau and Catherine Hetternix, widow of Pierre Houx, who died at Natchez.

26 March 1726

VALERIEN CAQUAU—native of Monterau, diocese of Sens in Bourgogne, son of Valerien Caquau and Magdelaine L'Enfant and MARIE BARBE KITTLER—native of Ara in the duchy of Vitemberg, widow of Andre Veleu (?), who died at the German Coast.

THE NEW ORLEANS FRENCH

15 September 1727

BERTRAND CARDINAL—resident of this parish, native of Villemarie
in Canada, son of deceased Jacques Cardinal and Louise Arrivée and
MARIE BRUNET—daughter of Jean Brunet dit Bourbonnais, resident
of Illinois and Elizabeth de Haye of the parish of Kaskaskia in Illinois.
Signed: Elizabeth Deshayes.

10 May 1723

NICOLAS CARDON and MARIE MICHEL DE BERNON.

8 August 1720

JEAN CARITON—native of Paris, son of Antoine Cariton and Catherine
Francoise Bailly and MARIE ANNE DINAN—native of Paris, daughter
of Jac Dinan, master second-hand dealer, and deceased Marie Therese
Passera.

20 March 1721

JEAN CARON—son of Louis Caron and Marguerite Duhamel and ANNE
MONI—daughter of Simon Moni and Francoise Pelletier.

2 February 1726

JACQUES CARRIERE surnamed [surnommé] (sic) Malogé—son of
deceased André Carriere of Montreal and Cecille Jannot of the diocese
of Quebec and MARIE FRANCOISE BABIN—daughter of deceased
Pierre Babin and Francoise Jallot, wife of Francois Carriere, resident of
this parish.

19

25 September 1730

JOSEPH CASTEL—widow of deceased Jacqueline Pinard, who died at New Orleans, native of the bishopric of Tournay, parish of Troye, son of Antoine Castel and MARIE CHOUPPE—who knows neither her birthplace nor her parents.

6 July 1721

LOUIS JOSEPH CASTEL—son of Antoine Castel and Marie Anne Masson and JACQUELINE PINARD—daughter of Francois Pinard and Genevieve Pinard (sic).

2 January 1720

LOUIS FRANCOIS CATTEL—master edge-tool maker, son of deceased Francois Cattel and Anne Lormet, native of the parish of Hamars, bishopric of Bayeux, province of Normandie and CHARLOTTE LE ROUX—daughter of Renault le Roux and René Pastique, native of L'Orient, parish of St. Louis, bishopric of Vannes, widow of Martin Chopier, who died at Pleinbouef.

25 May 1723

CHARLES CAYEUX—native of St. Germain in Lais, son of Francois Cayeux and Marie Gerin and CATHERINE PARISIS—daughter of Pierre Parisis and Catherine Savary, native of Paris, parish of St. Nicolas des Champs.

7 July 1722

ETIENNE CHANIO—son of Barthelemy Chanio and René Baudry, widower of Marie Rondeau, native of Ste. Sole, bishopric of La Rochelle and **JEANNE POUILLOT**—daughter of Thomas Pouillot and Marie Bouché, widow of Jean Marchand, native of Poissy, diocese of Chartres.

20 May 1727

JOSEPH CHAPERON—native of Montreal, diocese of Quebec, son of deceased Jacques Chaperon and Cecille Carriere and **MARIE LOUIS LE COQ**—native of Havre, diocese of Ro- - an (?), daughter of Francois Le Coq and Susanne Desmonts.

8 April 1723

CLAUDE CHARLES—native of Quinper and **JAQUETTE CULIOT**—native of Meluy.

30 April 1721

JACQUES CHARPENTIER—son of Jacques Charpentier and Marguerite Martin and **MARIE ANNE FETRE**—daughter of Pierre Fetre and Catherine Vincent.

6 August 1721

JEAN CHARPILLON—son of Leonard Charpillon and Charlotte [Blank] and **CHARLOTTE COUTURIER**—daughter of Jean Baptiste Couturier and Elizabeth Le Fevre.

THE NEW ORLEANS FRENCH

30 January 1730

FRANCOIS CHASTANG—Inspector of the commercial papers of the Company of the Indies, son of Francois Chastang, Secretary-in-Chief of the Presidial and Seneschal of Ninne (?) [Nimmes ?], and deceased Jeanne Charot and **ELIZABETH DAUVERGNE**—daughter of deceased Nicolas Dauvergne, bourgeois of Paris, and Catherine Richer, native of the parish of St. Roche.

27 May 1726

JOSEPH CHAUVIN DE LERY—native of Montreal, widower of Hypolite Mercier, who died at La Rochelle and **FRANCOISE LAURENCE LE BLANC**—daughter of deceased Henry Le Blanc and Seruanne Lemarie, native of St. Laurent, diocese of St. Malo.

4 May 1722, Fort Louis

NICOLAS CHEMIT—native of Alzace, worker for the Company and **MARIE FRANCOISE POLERY**—widow of Pierre (?) Philbert, native of the Fort de Kuel near Strabourg.

13 April 1722

JEAN BAPTISTE CHENIER—son of Jean Baptiste Chenier and Jeanne Descormier and **CATHERINE DUBY**—daughter of Jean Louis Duby and Marie Roger, widow of Pierre Francois Daublin.

20 May 1722

JACQUES CHESNIER—son of Jean Baptiste Chesnier and Jeanne Descormier, native of Montreal, Canada and **ELIZABETH LUCE**—daughter of Pierre Luce and Marie Jeanne Dubois of Donkerque.

22

THE NEW ORLEANS FRENCH

15 May 1727

LAURENT CHEURTY—native of Vierge (?) Le Francois, diocese of Chalons sur Marne, son of Jacques Cheurty and deceased Jeanne Morlay, soldier in the Company of Mr. Mandeville and **ANNE BLEIGNOT**—native of Gilien, diocese of Orleans, daughter of deceased Charles Bleignot and Marie Ducroe, widow of Jacques Castan.

12 October 1732

ANTOINE CLERMONT called St. Antoine—sergeant in the company of Mr. Renault, native of Naples, widower of Marie Jeanne Villiotte, who died at L'Orient and **SUSANNE MEITZ**—native of Keistatte (?), widow of Joseph Rister (or Kisler), who died in Louisiana.

31 December 1725

FRANCOIS COLIN—native of Langoumois, diocese of Angouleme, habitant of the Houmas, son of Joseph Colin, laborer, and Marie Gallard and **MARIE THEREZE DUPRE**—widow of Cabassier, while living, habitant of New Orleans, daughter of Louis Duprez, . . . [illegible] at Hennebon and Jeanne Briant, native of the bishopric of Vannes in Brittany.

4 October 1730

FRANCOIS CORSET [possibly Conée] native of Paris, parish of St. Germain Lauxerois, son of Maturin Corsée and Catherine Vivante and **ELIZABETH BIENVENU**—native of Dozanne [or Ozanne], canton of Berne, daughter of Jacques Bienvenu and Suzanne.

THE NEW ORLEANS FRENCH

6 July 1733

JEAN FLEURANT COSSÉ–son of Pierre Cossé and Vincente Le Boileu, native of Oree [or Orce], bishopric of Vannes and MARIE LAISAINE–daughter of deceased Dider Laisaine and Marie Tournelle, native of Miliza, bishopric of St. Paul of Lion.

27 April 1723

PIERRE COUGNON–native of Savoy and MARIE POITEVINE–native of Poitou.

9 August 1728

JOSEPH MARIE COUPLIN–native of Turin, son of Dominique Couplin and Angelique Marie de Liberat, now a sailor in the service of the Company of the Indes and LOUISE ROBERT QUARANTAY–native of the bishopric of Vannes, daughter of Robert Quarantay and Marie Goneganne, widow of Jean Monjienes (?), who died in Louisiana.

27 June 1721

JACQUES COURTABLEAU–son of Jean Courtableau and Jeanne Chapoupeau and CATHERINE MENU–daughter of Jean Menu and Marie Francoise Boisseau.

27 October 1727

JEAN BAPTISTE CRESLY–native of Besancon, parish of St. Magdelaine, wet cooper, son of Pierre Francois Cresly and Georgine Chevalier and MARIE FRANCOISE AYETTE–native of Quimperlé, daughter of Francois Ayette and Jeanne Paulet, bourgeois of that place, of the parish of St. Colomban.

24

11 January 1726

JEAN CRETZMAN—renounces the heresy of Calvinism, the religion in which he was born and reared, native of the canton of Berne, Switzerland, widower of Barbe Hostman who died at the German Coast and **SUZANNE ROMMEL**—daughter of deceased Henry Rommel and Ursule ————— .

7 October 1726

JEAN JACQUES CRETZMAN—son of André Cretzman and Jacqueline Rehebin of this parish and **CATHERINE MUNICHEZ (?)**—daughter of Jean Pierre Municher and deceased Barbe Hilperté, of the German Coast.

9 July 1727

FRANCOIS CROIX dit MACHEATERRE—soldier of the Company of Mr. Demandeville, major, native of Basse Normandy, diocese of Rhouan, son of Giles Croix and Marie Grandin and **FRANCOISE LEFLOT**—native of Chateauneuf in Basse Bretagne, bishopric of Cornuaille, daughter of René Leflot and Marguerite Daniel.

17 January 1726

JEAN FRANCOIS CRONIER—habitant of Natchitoches, son of Louis Cronier, carpenter, and Anne Vignon, bourgeois at Fonnet, diocese of Langres and **MARIE SOUSSE**—daughter of Philippe Sausse, bourgeois of Etelein near Alberque and Anne Martiez.

30 May 1723

MR. ETIENNE DALCOUR—native of Bordeau, son of Mr. Dalcourt, lawyer in parliament and Dlle. Catherine Godefroy and **MLLE. MARIE JOSEPH TRUDEAU**—native of New Orleans, daughter of Marie Trudeau and Jeanne Burelle.

7 May 1731

FRANCOIS ANTOINE DAMARON—druggist, native of St. Germain en Laye, archbishopric of Paris, son of Antoine Damaron, King's Druggist, and Jeanne Amour, widower of Catherine Duchemin and **FRANCOISE TREPANIE**—daughter of Claude Trepanier, resident, and Genevieve Burelle.

17 April 1730

PIERRE d'ARJAT—[Ed. note—This record is garbled. One Pierre Drigny is mentioned and may be the major party. Whoever he is, he is a native of Tilly in Lorraine, bishopric of Verdun.] and **ANNE ADAM**—daughter of Jean Adam and Marguerite Alos, native of Platée, bishopric of Trilly in Brittany, widow of Simon Gilbert, who died at Natchez.

15 November 1720, New Biloxi

Certification of the marriage of **NICOLAS DARTELLO**—native of Metz in Loraine and **CATHERINE LIGNE**—native of the diocese of Breste.

4 January 1723

FRANCOIS CONTANT DASTI—worker, son of Nicolas Darti and Jeanne Bidort and **MARGUERITE DOUTRICOURT**—daughter of Pierre Dautricourt and Agnes Perussy.

21 November 1726

VALENTIN JOSEPH DAUBLIN—master maker of edge-tools, native of Monbillord, archbishopric of Cambray, son of Gilles Daublin and Catherine Bouillet and **MARIE MARGUERITE JOSEPH DECUIR**—native of Macon, archbishopric of Cambray, daughter of Albert Decuire and Catherine Doner, residents of Pointe Coupée.

THE NEW ORLEANS FRENCH

29 May 1730

ANTOINE DAUMAS—native of Ré in Provence, son of Francois Daumas and Marie Piete Renard and **ANNE MARIE VAU**—native of Hago, daughter of Gaspard Vau and Anne.

20 November 1731

JEAN FRANCOIS DAUPHIN—resident on the upper river, native of Meziere, archbishopric of Rheims in Champagne, widower of Jeanne Gerandalle, who died in Louisiana and **JEANNE DU CHEMIN**—native of Chaumont in Bassigny, bishopric of Langres, parish of St. Jean, daughter of Edmé Du Chemin and Catherine La Forest.

19 November 1725

JEAN JOSEPH DAUPHIN—native of Mezieres, diocese of Rheims, son of Jean Francois Dauphin and Jeanne Gerandalle and **ELIZABETH BIRQUENMAYER**—native of the diocese of Espire, daughter of deceased Gaspart Birquenmayer and deceased Marie Barbe.

29 May 1732

JEAN JOSEPH DAUPHIN—native of Cherleville, archbishopric of Rheims, widower of Jeanne Bernardin, who died in Louisiana and **ANNE MARIE MUNIE**—native of Spir, widow of Henry, who died in Louisiana.

17 February 1727

JOSEPH DAUPHIN—habitant of Cannes Bruslees, widower of Marie Libeth Birkmaire who died here, son of J. Francois Dauphin and Jeanne Gerandac (?) and **MARIE ANNE BERNARDIN**—daughter of Jean Bernardin and Adrienne Martin, native of Berne in Switzerland.

10 February 1732

LAURENT DAVID—son of Guillaume David and Perine Riaut, native "D'Erdon," parish of St. Pierre, bishopric of Vannes and **JEANNE FRANCOISE DAUPHIN**—daughter of Jean Francois Dauphin and Jeanne Gerandalle, native of Charleville, parish of St. Remy, diocese of Rheims.

3 February 1733

LAURENT DAVID—master mason, native of Vennes in Brittany, widower of Jeanne Francoise Dauphin, who died in Louisiana and **MARIE FRANCOISE MANNE**—native of Arles in Provence, son of Francois Mannes and Elizabeth Chelet.

15 May 1725

JEAN DE BELMAST [or Belmart] —sailor of the Company and **MARIE ELEQ**—native of the parish of Brie, bishopric of Hemelon, daughter of Pierre Eleq and Elizabeth Pommier [possibly Poinier], bourgeoise.

28 March 1731

CEZAIRE DE BLANC—lieutenant of the Royal Regiment of the Infantry of the Marine, native of Marseille in Provence, son of deceased Nobleman Charles De Blanc, captain of the Champagne Regiment, and deceased Dame Marguerite D'Espannet and **ELIZABETH GRIOL**—native of Toulon in Provence, daughter of Pierre Griol, while living, King's Engineer, and Therese Beyle, widow of Monsieur Delarmas, while living, King's Commissioner in Louisiana.

THE NEW ORLEANS FRENCH

12 January 1732

LOUIS DE BREUIL VILLARS—native of Paris, son of Sieur Joseph Dubreuil Villars, Concessioner at Chopitoulas, and Marie Payen and **FELICTE DE LA CHAISE**—native of Nantes, Brittany, daughter of deceased Mr. de la Chaise, heretofore King's Commissioner and General Director of the Colony, and Marguerite Cailly. Mr. Prat is her tutor.

25 February 1721, Old Biloxi

JEAN DE BRY—son of Mr. Manuel de Bry, *procureur du Roy* en l'Election de la Vale de Lion and Dame Antoinelle (*sic*) Motenchon (?) and **CHARLOTTE CATHERINE BOIRON**—daughter of deceased Etienne Boiron, lieutenant in Duzan's regiment, and Helene Catherine Vondrebek.

21 March 1730

JEAN BAPTISTE DE CHAVANE—native of Paris, parish of St. Paul, son of deceased Paul de Chavane, Commissioner of Wars, and deceased Marthe Roussau, widower of Jacqueline Petit, who died at Natchitoches and **THEREZE FICHOUX**—native of St. Malo, parish of St. Seruax (?), widow of Master Guillaume Loengueray, while living Royal Notary at St. Malo. He died at the Fort of St. Pierre de la Martinique. She is the daughter of deceased Jacques Fichoux, who was a ship's captain while living, and Gillette Rossert (?).

5 August 1727

MONSIEUR JOACHIM DE GAUNERY [possibly Gauvery] —Captain of a Company of the Marine, widower of Marie Anne de l'Estrier, who died in Louisiana and **CATHERINE DE L'ESTRIER PIERRE** (*sic*)—native of Besancon, widow of Justin Guouim (?), who died in Louisiana. Signed by: Mr. de Perrier, commandant-general of the province; Mr. de la Chaise, the King's Commissioner, and Mr. de la Boulee, *beaufrere* of the bride.

THE NEW ORLEANS FRENCH

No Date—probably late April or early May 1722

ETIENNE d'EGLE—son of Jean Degle and Marie Pradeau, native of Beauport, diocese of Quebec and **SUSANE d'ESPERON**—daughter of [Blank] d'Esperon and Marie Fouchard.

25 November 1732

RAYMOND ST. MARTIN DE JARQUIBERY—heretofore guardian of the storehouse for the militia, son of Arnaud de Jorequibery and Marie Resalt (??), native of Demezain (?), bishopric of Baipme (?) and **MARIE BRUSLEE**—native of Dauphin Island, daughter of Antoine Philippe Bruslée and Marthe Fremont, widow of Jean Dugay, who died in Louisiana.

26 February 1729

LOUIS MORISSET DE LA CHEMILLIERE—licensed in law, son of Gabriel Morisette and Dame Francoise Bonvin, of the parish of Chervieux (?), diocese of Poitier and **FRANCOISE MARTIN**—widow of Antoine de la Joye.

9 November 1726

NICOLAS DE LA COUR—son of Antoine de la Cour and Francoise Duclos, residents of St. Jean des Champs, bishopric of Contance [or Contanee], parishoner of Natchez and **PERINE BRETTE**—daughter of deceased Louis Brette and Isabelle Roy. The father died at Mobile. Perine Brette is a parishoner at New Orleans.

THE NEW ORLEANS FRENCH

3 November 1728

ANTOINE DELATTE—son of Pierre Delatte and Catherine de la Garde, native of Doy, bishopric of Aras and **MARGUERITE LE JEUNE**— daughter of Claude le Jeune, mareschal by profession, native of the parish of Cartelheim [or Castelheim] and Cristine Colson, daughter of Dominique Colson and Anne Marie Kidt, of the parish of Artorfs (?) in Lorraine. [Ed. note—This record seems to be garbled and contains parts of another record; however, it was copied as it stands in the original.]

31 August 1733

JEAN DELEBAT—son of Jean Delebat and Marie Dereson, native of Port Louis, bishopric of Vannes and **VICTORIE VIALENT**—widow of deceased Nicolas Humbert, native of Boulaine, bishopric of St. Paul, daughter of Laurent Vialent and Jacquette Dauaude.

10 December 1731

MONSIEUR BARTHELEMY DE MARIOL, esquire, Seigneur de la Massonne et de Lormeau—Ensign of the King's ships, son of deceased Monsieur Francois de Mariol, esquire, Lieutenant of the King's ships, and Jeanne Heurtin, of the parish of Rochefort, diocese of La Rochelle and **ANNE FRANCOISE SALMON**—minor daughter of Monsieur Edmé Gatien Salmon, Commissioner of the Marine, Ordonnateur in the province of Louisiana, and Anne Francoise de Mergery, native of the parish of Viller St. Jacques, diocese of Sens.

23 April 1721

ANTOINE d'ENGREMONT—Son of Jean d'Engremont and Nicole Tessier and **GENEVIEVE MANDRE**—daughter of Louis Mandre and Charlotte Henry.

31

THE NEW ORLEANS FRENCH

10 February 1721, Old Biloxi

NOEL DE PROUOND—son of Jean de Prouond and Claudine Amar, native of Lyon, now a resident of Mirangouin and **LOUISE VOLLERY.**

13 April 1733

JEAN FRANCOIS DEROZE—drummer for the Swiss in the company of Monsieur Merveilleuse, native of Vienne, son of Jean Francois Deroze and Elizabeth Bauer and **GENEVIEVE DERBO**—widow of deceased Ebert Fundelick, daughter of Augustin Derbo and Marguerite Pipe.

23 February 1729

JOSEPH DES CHAMPS—son of Louis des Champs and Isabel Colin, native of Lugny sur Marne, parish of La Magdelaine, bishopric of Meaux in Brie and **MARIE MAGDELAINE BOURU**—daughter of Guillaume Bouru and Genevieve de Riant, widow of Etienne Barasson, native of Montargy, parish of La Magdelaine, bishopric of Sem in Bourgogne.

3 January 1726

JOSEPH DESCHAMPS—native of Logny in Brie, diocese of Brie, custodian of charters for the Company, widower of Claudine Guenet, who died at Cannes Brusle and **JEANNE VEILLY**—native of Cornouailles, widow of Jean Bouillon called Potvin, soldier in Mr. D'Artaguette's company who died here.

28 May 1722

MESSIRE FRANCOIS DES COUBLANT—escuyer, Seigneur Gilbaut, son of Messire Charles Descoublan, escuyer, Seigneur de la Rousseliere and Dame Marguerite d'Illerin, native of St. Laurent de Boue, bishopric

of La Rochelle and **MAGDELAINE ROY**—daughter of Mr. Francois
Roy and Dame Marie Vince(n)te, native of the parish of St. Louis of
Rochefort, widow of Mr. Jacques Delury, escuyer, Sieur de Verrasac,
officer in His Magesty's troops. [Among the signers were: Decoublant,
Duplessy, and Tonty.]

13 April 1722

JEAN FRANCOIS DE ST. AMAN DESPIE—son of Jacque Despie and
Dominique Bordeliere and **MARIE FRANCOISE DU BUISSON**—daughter of Leon du Buisson and Marie Anne Carron.

26 June 1730

MANO (?) DE TRONQUILLY—esquire, son of Main (?) de Tronquilly,
esquire, and Francoise Varin, native of St. Brieux, widower of Marie
Chartier, who died in Louisiana and **MARIE JOSEPH LEMAIRE**—
daughter of Jean Lemaire, captain of the King's Bodyguard, and Marie
du Valois, widow of Francois de Fontaine, Comptroler of the Royal
Hospitals.

4 April 1721

PIERRE DE VAUVRAY—son of Jean de Vauvray and Francoise
Jeofournais (?) and **MAGDELAINE BOULOGNE**—daughter of Pierre
Boulogne and Jeanne Tessier.

5 January 1723

JEAN PIERRE DE VIAU—son of Jean de Viau and Marguerite Chapu,
native of Chevremont, diocese of Bezancon and **JEANNE MARIE BOIS**
—daughter of Berthelemy Bois and Danis Laclet, native of Bissort [or
Biffort].

THE NEW ORLEANS FRENCH

8 June 1722

CLAUDE DIDIER—son of Claude Didier and Marie Varenne, native of St. George in the bishopric of Dupuy in Vivarais and MARIE STRISKER —daughter of Jean Strisker and Anne Elizabeth [Blank], native of Alsace.

4 February 1727

FRANCOIS DIEUDONNE—goldsmith, native of Namm (?) in Flanders, son of [Blank] Dieudonné, *fonder marchand*, and *Dame* Delfone and CATHERINE NOTACHE—daughter of Jean Jacques Notache, deceased, and Catherine Trouillet, wife of Jean Soubamier, resident of Gentilly.

14 October 1733

FRANCOIS DIEUDONNE—founder, widower of Marie Ducoste, who died at Natchez, native of Namur in Flanders, son of Dieudonné, founder, and Anne De Fosse and ELIZABETH HOMMAR—widow of Nicolas Henry, who died in Louisiana, daughter of Louis Hommar and Elizabeth Caija, native of Neuy St. Fron, bishopric of Soissons in Picardy.

12 January 1728

GASPART DILLY—native of Alsace, son of Jacob Dilly and Barbe Oswald, widower of Elizabeth Stuzlé, who died in Louisiana and BARBE KEIDEL—daughter of Jean Keidel and Eve Schnazberg, widow of Jean George Bretz, who died in Louisiana.

24 February 1721

PIERRE DIROUCHE—son of Cristophe Dirouche and Jeanne Cologne and CATHERINE DELAUNAY—daughter of Claude Delauney and Magdelaine Veau.

34

THE NEW ORLEANS FRENCH

28 October 1727

Consent of Mr. de la Chaise for the marriage of **DOMINIQUE** and **MARIE ANNE**, two Negroes who belong to him.

20 September 1723

FRANCOIS PHILIPPE DONNE—native of Louarde in Flanders, son of Sebastien Donné and Marie Magdelaine Barre and **MARIE ANNE ANDRE**—native of Melbergen Touslach, daughter of Jean Andre and Anne Marie [Blank].

5 May 1722

CLAUDE DORMOIS—native of the parish of Faverné in Flanders, carpenter for the Company and **MARIE LOUISE CATO**—widow of Charles Bernard, native of the parish of Bournin (?), bishopric of Boulogne.

19 May 1722, Fort Louis

JEAN MARTIN DORUILLIERS—native of the bishopric of Troye in Champagne and **RENE CHARBONNETTE**—native of La Rochelle, parish of Notre Dame.

2 June 1721

PIERRE FRANCOIS DOUBLIN—son of Gilles Doublin and Catherine Bouille and **CATHERINE DUBY**—daughter of Jean Louis Duby and Marie Roger.

35

17 November 1732

MATURIN DREUX—resident of Gentilly, officer in the militia of this province, son of deceased Louis Dreux, bourgeois of Savigny Souvillé and Francois Harant, native of Savigny Souvillé, diocese of Angers and CLAUDINE FRANCOISE HUGOT—daughter of deceased Jean Hugot, while living, guardian of the storehouse at the concession of Monsieur Le Blanc, and Francoise Martin, now wife of Sieur Morisset.

28 April 1733

PIERRE DREUX—officer of the militia, son of Louis Dreux and Francoise Harand, native of the parish of Savigny in Anjou, diocese of Anger and ANNE CORBIN BACHEMIN—daughter of Jean Corbin and Anne Marie Judith Le Hardis, native of St. Malo, parish of St. Laurent.

10 May 1728

ANTOINE DRIGNY—native of Commeray in Lorraine, bishopric of Toul, *coutellier,* son of Nicolas Drigny and Catherine Morette and JEANNE BOURGEOIS—daughter of Antoine Bourgeois and Catherine Louillon, native of Maran, bishopric of La Rochelle, widow of Jacques Coquelin dit La Forme, who died in Louisiana.

17 January 1725

LOUIS DRULHON—native of Maletauerne, parish of St. André, bishopric of Dalais, son of deceased Pierre Drulhon and Anne Corhesace, while living, his father was a tailor, residing in a village named La Serre and MARIE FRANCOISE HERO—native of Landernau, parish of St. Cardon, daughter of deceased Joseph Hero and Marie Anne Frené, while living, her father was a bourgeois in Landerneau.

THE NEW ORLEANS FRENCH

6 May 1721

JOSEPH DUBRO—son of Jean Baptiste Dubro and Marguerite Descros and **MARGUERITE BELANGER**—daughter of Jacques Belanger and Catherine Garboise.

20 January 1728

NICOLAS DUCRAY—native of Conflan in Savoie, son of Jean Claude du Cray and Jeanne Chappé, soldier in the Company of Mr. D'Artaguet and **PERRINE HUET**—daughter of Mathurin Huet and Thomasse Lemay, native of St. Juan (*sic*), bishopric of St. Malo.

1 March 1729

NICOLAS DUCRET [or Dueret ?]—master shoemaker, son of Jean Ducret (?), master shoemaker, and Jeanne Chapet, native of Conflan in Savoy, widower of Perine Huet, who died in Louisiana and **MARIE LOUISE CATEAU**—daughter of Francois Cateau and Francoise Totin, native of Bourvin (?), bishopric of Boulogne, widow of Claude Dormois called Compton, who died in Louisiana.

26 February 1726

LOUIS DUGES—native of the diocese of Cahors, surgeon, son of Pierre Duges and Marguerite Legarde and **MARGUERITE THERESE PIERREMOND**—native of St. Remis, duchy of Luxembourg, bishopric of Treves, widow of deceased Valentin Canelle, who died at the parish of Mobile. Among the witnesses were Jacques Croustelhas, Michel Rossard, secretary of the Superior Council, Pierre Manadet, surgeon, and Bernard Alex Vielle, surgeon.

THE NEW ORLEANS FRENCH

2 April 1731

JEAN DUGUAY—native of St. Cent Florin de Monzon, bishopric of Vienna (?) in Dauphiné, son of Jacques Duguay and Jeanne Benard and MARIE BRUSLEE—native of Dauphin Island, daughter of Philippe Antoine Brusleé and Marthe Fremont.

25 June 1727

ALAIN DUGUE—native of Rennes in Bretagne, son of deceased Alain Dugué and Jeanne Morelle and ANGELIQUE GIRARDY—daughter of Joseph Girardy and Francoise Indienne.

2 April 1731

GILBERT DUMAS—native of Paris, parish of St. Benoist, son of Gabriel Dumas and Marguerite Dumon, widower of Claudine Sarazin, who died at Mobile and MARIE HAUSCORNE—daughter of Jean Hauscorne and Marguerite Polette, native of Rouen, parish of St. Lau.

1 March 1729

JEAN DUMAST called Beausejour—soldier in the Company of D'Artaguette, native of Dorat in Basse Marche, bishopric of Limoges, son of Antoine Dumast and Francoise Chambly and MARIE LA RESILIERE—native of Besson (??), bishopric of Leon in L'Annois, widow of Nicolas Cardon, who died in Louisiana.

19 April 1730

FRANCOIS BINJAMIN DUMONT called Montigny—ex-lieutenant, son of Jacques Dumont, lawyer in the Parliament of Paris, and Francois Lemare, native of Paris, parish of St. Come and MARIE BARON—daughter of Jacques Baron, bourgeois of Morlin, and Marie Legras, widow of Jean Roussin, who died at Natchez.

THE NEW ORLEANS FRENCH

5 November 1720, Old Fort Biloxi

AUGUSTIN DUPART—pilot of St. Malo and CATHERINE BOYARD—
native of the parish of St. Jacques de la Boucherie de Paris.

30 August 1723

CHARLES DUPONT—soldier in the Natchitoches garrison, company
of Mr. de Barnaval, son of Simon Dupont, native of the parish of Ste.
Croix, diocese of Paris and MARIE MARGUERITE FRANCOISE—
daughter of Isaac (*sic*), native of Metz.

31 March 1721

JACQUES DUPONT—son of Claude Dupont and Magdelaine Eloy and
MARIE ANNE FOUCAULT—daughter of Jean Foucault and Nicole
Francois Defer.

6 June 1725

JACQUES DUPREZ—native of Caen in Normandy, parish of St. Pierre,
son of Guillaume Duprez and Rene Andre, *menuissier* and MAGDE-
LAINE MERCIER—native of Rheims in Champagne, parish of St.
Etienne, daughter of Jean Baptiste Mercier and Louise Bourgeois, widow
of Simon La Caille, who died in this parish.

24 May 1728

GASPARD DUPS—native of the canton of Zurich in Switzerland, son of
Jacob Dups and Anne [Blank], widower of Marguerite Kettliger (?),
who died at the German Coast and MARIE BARBE KITTELER—native
of the duchy of Vitemberg, daughter of Jean Mathieu Kitteler and
Marguerite [Blank], widow of Valerien Caquau, who died at the German Coast.

39

THE NEW ORLEANS FRENCH

10 February 1721

PIERRE DURAND—son of Jerome Durand and Marguerite Blanchard, native of Maran in Poitou, now a resident of Illinois and **FRANCOIS RABU.**

21 April 1727

EITENNE DURANTE—Sergeant, widower of "facée," who died in this parish and **MARIE RICHARD**—native of Cholet, diocese of Augers.

29 June 1721

PAUL DURIF—soldier, native of Clermont in Auvergne and **MARIE CURE**—native of Ste. Thereze.

25 November 1720, Biloxi

DENYS DUTROU—native of the parish of St. Sulpice, diocese of Paris and **MARIE JOSEPHE GRACE,** native of the parish of St. Hubert, country of Artois.

27 December 1726

NICOLAS DUVAUX—son of Alexandre Duvau, native of Paris, parish of St. Laurent and **GENEVIEVE GOYER**—widow of Gaspart, native of Chalon in Champagne.

THE NEW ORLEANS FRENCH

29 December 1733

MONSIEUR BERNARD DUVERGES—former lieutenant, King's Engineer, son of Monsieur Francois Artus Duverges, officer in the regiment of Bandes (?) Granmontoises, and Marie Lagrenade, native of the parish of Eurt, in the country of La Bour, bishopric of Bayonne and **MARIE THERESE PINAU**—daughter of Monsieur Pierre Pinau and Susanne Munier, native of La Rochelle, parish of St. Sauveur, bishopric of La Rochelle.

25 November 1720, Biloxi

JACQUES DUVOEL—native of the parish of Vitry sur Seine, diocese of Paris and **MARIE LOUISE BALIVEL**—native of St. Germain en Lay.

3 January 1733

JACQUES ENOUL DE LIVAUDAIS—captain of the port, son of Jacques Esnould and Marie Le Jaloux, native of St. Malo in Brittany and **MARIE GENEVIEVE LA SOURCE**—native of Mobile, daughter of Pierre Babin La Source and Francoise Jalotte.

3 February 1728

FRANCOIS FAUCHER—native of Vry, bishopric of Nantes, son of Jacques Faucher and Charlotte Morelle, soldier in the Company of Renaud and **MARIE ANNE GIARD**—native of Paris, parish of St. Gilles, daughter of Antoine Giard and Michelle Gosselein, widow of Jean Bastien dit Baguette, who died in Louisiana.

1 July 1721

Dispensed with the last ban, with the permission of Mr. Davion, Grand Vicar.
JEAN FEUILLE—native of the parish of Mondragon, diocese of Orange, widower of Suzanne Chambouille, son of Francois Feuille and Jeanne Venissard and ROSE MAZERE—widow of Louis Bernard, daughter of Guillaume Mazere and Claude Bosanne.

28 August 1731

ETIENNE FILSASSIER—goldsmith, native of Paris, parish of St. Germain Le Vieux, son of Michel Filassier and Magdelaine Trainblet [or Trainllet] and MARIE ADRIENNE VUITRIQUIN—native of Maubuche, daughter of Francois Vuitriquin and Charlotte Hegue.

4 May 1722

NICOLAS FISO [or Fino]—native of Paris, parish of St. Denis and MARIE ANNE LEGARÉ—native of Mastrick, parish of St. Antoine.

4 February 1721

ALBERT FONDELAY—German soldier in the company of Mr. Le Blanc and GENEVIEVE DERO.

29 October 1720

Certification of the priest at Old Fort Biloxi on the marriage of ALBERT FONDELIN and MARIE ELIZABETH OLERIEN.

17 February 1721

Certification of the marriage of **CLAUDE FONTAINE**—soldier in the Co. of Mr. de Monmor (?) and **MARIE VIBER**—widow of Francois Posan.

13 December 1723

CLAUDE FONTAINE—native of Lemai, bishopric of Rhouan, previously married to Marie Vilien, resident of this town and **MARIE ANNE HAUCHECORNE** (?)—native of Rouan, parish of St. Cloud, widow of David Jannot, smelter in Lorraine, of the Company of the Indies.

23 April 1721

JEAN BAPTISTE FONTAINE—son of André Fontaine and Marie Suet and **LOUISE LEGUIN**—daughter of Paul Leguin and Catherine Fleche.

24 January 1725

PIERRE FRANCOIS FONTAINE—native of Brunemont, diocese of Aras, son of deceased Francois Fontaine and Jeanne Aigo, while living the father was a habitant of Brunemont and **JEANNE LE BIHANT**—native of Hennebon, diocese of Vannes, daughter of deceased Michel Behan, bourgeois of Hennebon, and Joachim Gourlin.

22 February 1725

DOMINIQUE FORETS—native of Gée, "frontiere" of Switzerland, bishopric of Besancon, corporal in the company of Mr. de Merveilleux and **FRANCOISE BOUCHE**—native of Rhennes, in Brittany.

43

THE NEW ORLEANS FRENCH

13 November 1720, Old Fort Biloxi

RENE FOUCAULT and **MARIE ANDRELY.**

26 July 1721

PIERRE FOURE—son of Pierre Fouré and Rene Salone and **LOUISE MIRE**—daughter of Jean Miré and Marie Thereze Le Roy.

6 August 1720

JEAN FOURNIER—native of St. Laurent du Pont, bishopric of Grenoble in Dauphiné, son of deceased Enne Fournier and Jeanne Guichon and **MARIE ANNE RABOUIN**—native of St. Germain in Lay, daughter of Guillaume Rabouin and Marie Claude Loudien [or Houdier].

16 August 1728

Marriage of two Negroes, **FRANCOIS** and **MARIE**, who belong to Tixerant.

15 November 1728

JEAN FREDERIC called La Fontaine—drummer in the Company of De Gauvry, native of Moulin in Bourbonnais, son of deceased Jean Frederic and Marie Le Cahussé de Brunelle and **MARIE ISBETTE**—native of Douay, daughter of Charles La Vallée and Marie Christienne.

12 March 1721

PIERRE FUGERE—son of Jean Fugere and Noel Le Clair and **ETIE-NETTE GENE**—daughter of Antoine Gené and Nicol Frezot.

THE NEW ORLEANS FRENCH

6 August 1723

JEAN FUMA—native of Mondragon in Provence, widower of Isabo Manne and **JEANNE RONNADE**—native of Boulains in the "Comté of Avignon," widow of Moray.

14 July 1722

JEAN FUMAT—native of the parish of Mondragon in Provence, worker for the Company and **JEANNE ELIZABETH RICHARDE**—widow of Francois Mane.

27 January 1723

LOUIS GAL called Boutonnier—soldier and **MARIE RICHARD**—native of Melun in Brie, widow of deceased Aman.

8 August 1730

FRANCOIS GENOUI—master carpenter, native of the bishopric of Vannes, son of Laurent Genoui and Marguerite Le Mendeque, widower of Catherine Picou, who died at Biloxi and **PERINE NEZET**—native of Kiantique, bishopric of Vannes.

15 January 1725

LAURENT GHETZ—native of Lingin, diocese of Spire, son of Frederic Ghetz and Suzanne Metz and **ELIZABETH BAILLY**—native of Loraine, daughter of Claude Bailly and Francoise Corrié. Both have been living in this parish for several years. Joseph Ritter is "beaupere" of the groom.

6 February 1731

ANTOINE GILBERT called la Montagne—son of Pierre Gilbert and Marie Bienheureuse, native of Dupuis in La Velez, "frontiere de Dauvergne (*sic*)" and **JEANNE LE GUIDER**—daughter of Jean Le Guider and Genton Grillon, native of Quimper, widow of a soldier named Languedoc.

26 April 1731

FRANCOIS GIN [in margin written Guin] —called Belle Rose—native of Niort in Poitou, son of Jean Gin and Jeanne Jouette, widower of Marguerite Boudin, who died at Mobile and **MATHERINE BLOCKERINE**—native of Stockheim, daughter of Laurent Blocker and Anne Marie, widow of Jean Aubrosse.

25 November 1728

ETIENNE GIRAULT—*menuisier*, native of D'Oleron, bishopric of Xainte, son of Bertrand Girault and Catherine Lemay (?) and **CATHERINE HULVOY**—native of L'Orient, bishopric of Vannes, widow of Michel Bonpain, daughter of Gilles Hulvoy and Jacquette Legourlay.

19 January 1733

MARTIN GODAR—*taillandier*, native of St. Denis, bishopric of Paris, son of Jean Baptiste Godar and Marie Le Pointier and **LOUISE FRANCOISE SAVARIE**—native of Dieppe, bishopric of Rouen, widow of Barthelemy Madré, who died in Louisiana.

THE NEW ORLEANS FRENCH

15 November 1728

LOUIS GODIN—resident of Natchez, native of Valet, diocese of Nantes, son of Pierre Godin, master tailor, and Gilberte Rouau [or Rouan] and JEANNE ELIZABETH COMBE—native of La Rochelle, parish of Notre Dame, daughter of Mathieu Combe, *maitre courer or couser* and Jeanne Roussaud.

17 May 1728

NICOLAS GOJOT called L'Esperance—soldier in the Company of D'Artaguet, native of Saremont, bishopric of Langre, son of Nicolas Gojot, laborer, and Didier Renaud and CATHERINE MERINE—native of Vorme, daughter of J. Merine and Dorothree Schat.

3 March 1722

JEAN BAPTISTE GON—Escuyer, sieur de la haute Maison, son of Mr. Pierre Francois Gon, Escuyer, and Dame Marie Anne Nouvel [or Novel] de Senoisville [or Fenonville] of Paris, parish of St. Paul and JACQUE-LINE LEPETIT—daughter of [Blank] Le Petit and Julienne Grolet.

16 June 1726

CLAUDE GONET—native of Genier [or Gevier] in Franche-Comté, diocese of Besancon, commander of the Negroes of the Company of the Indies and MARIE ANNE PREVOST—widow of Phillibert Froges (?), who died in Louisiana.

4 February 1722

FRANCOIS GOTRON—son of Michel Gotron and René Martine and OLINE LETARTAIZE—daughter of Julien Letartaize and Perine Potevin.

47

3 February 1733

FRANCOIS GOURNOUVEL called St. Anne–soldier in the company of Dauterive, native of Frindicque, bishopric of St. Malo, son of Roux Gournouvel and Julienne Gamu and **JACQUELINE CHAUMONT**–native of St. Germain Lauxerois, widow of Francois Dubie, who died at Natchez.

24 November 1721

JEAN GRENIER–native of Rouan, parish of St. André, son of Jean Grenier and Catherine Lemoiteux and **CATHERINE HOUARD**–widow of Jean Alain, daughter of Joseph Houart and Catherine Valin.

6 February 1733

MATHIEU GRUEL–native of Pledhieu, bishopric of Dole in Brittany, son of Francois Gruel and Julienne Le Marchand and **JULIENNE GAGNAR**–native of Hennebond, bishopric of Vannes, widow of Francois Vuitriquin, who died at Pointe Coupée.

5 (?) August 1726

AGNAN GUERIN DE LA BOULAY–native of Orleans, lieutenant of the infantry in the regiment of the Marine garrisoned at New Orleans, son of Alexandre Francoise Guerin, Seigneur de Brez, King's Councilor and Commissioner-General du Sailly d'Orleans, and Dame Marie Anne Simone de St. Albert and **JEANNE TRUDEAU**–daughter of Mr. Francois Trudeau and Dame Jeanne Burelle. Among the witnesses were Joseph Lassus de Marsilly, carpenter of the province, and Jean Perault, Commissioner of the King.

THE NEW ORLEANS FRENCH

4 June 1721

JACQUES GUERIN—son of Etienne Guerin and Jeanne Danue (?) and
CATHERINE ST. LAURENT—daughter of Francois St. Laurent and
Elizabeth Girard.

11 July 1730

PIERRE GUETRO—son of Bonnaventure Guetro and Marguerite Reitre,
native of Hennebond, parish of St. Gilles, bishopric of Vannes and
MARIE LOUISE MESCHIN called St. Germain—daughter of Louis
Mechin St. Germain and Louise Guioman [or Guiomar], native of
Hennebond, parish of St. Gilles, bishopric of Vannes.

7 April 1723

SIMON GUIGNARD—soldier in Barnoval's Company and CLAUDINE
GRISON.

12 April 1728

RODOLF GUILAN—son of deceased Pierre Guilan and Marie Bau- - - -et
(?), native of Mora, canton of Fribourg, habitant of the German Coast
and DOROTHE TZINECK—daughter of deceased Jacques Tzineck and
Marie Anne [last name unknown], also of the German Coast.

17 April 1730

LOUIS GUISEAU [or very possibly Guiscard] —resident of Natchez, son
of Jean G - - - and Marie Lamalatie, native of St. Portie, bishopric of
Montauban and MARIE COIGNARD—native of St. Martin de l'Isle de
Ré, bishopric of La Rochelle, daughter of Pierre Coignard and Marie
Bretonne, widow of Pierre Tonnitau (?) called le Blu, who died at
Natchez.

49

THE NEW ORLEANS FRENCH

23 February 1726

AUGUSTIN GUY—native of Amien, parish of St. Pierre, habitant "aux Cola- - (?)," son of Augustin Guy and Marie Hodouatte and **BARBE GOTREALLE**—widow of Jean Sidton (?) [or Pidton ?], heretofore resident of the German Coast, daughter of Jean Gotreal of Quintenille.

1 March 1729

JEAN LOUIS HAMELIN—native of Grondine, parish of St. Charles, bishopric of Quebec, son of Francois Hamelin and Marie Magdelaine Auber and **MARIE ANNE FOURNIER**—daughter of Jean Baptiste Fournier and René Vribault (?), native of La Rochelle, parish of St. Sauveur.

16 June 1721

JULIEN HARACE—son of Mathurin Harace and Anne Floein and **THEREZE MAISONETTE**—daughter of Antoine Maisonette and Marie Magdelaine Mathé [or Malhé].

19 May 1722, Fort Louis

FRANCOISE HERISSE—Drummer in the Company of Mr. Le Blanc, native of Chambly in Picardy and **MARIE CATHERINE RAFLON**—native of Paris, parish of St. Eustache, St. Denis Street. [The groom signed: Hericée.]

18 January 1724

JEAN BAPTISTE HOMARD—native of Nevilly St. Front, diocese of Soisson, habitant of Arkansas and **ANNE MARGUERITE MOSSEL**—native of Minden in Hanoves (?), widow of Jean Danfenteo (?).

5 June 1730

THOMAS HOS—Free Negro of Jamaica and JEANNE MARIE—"Negresse Libre de nation."

22 June 1722

NICOLAS HUBERT—locksmith on the concession of D'Artaguette and Benac, son of Nicolas Imbert and Sabastien Bajou, native of Bonhomme in Alsace and VICTOIRE VIALANCE—daughter of Laurent Lialance and Jacques Guichard.

5 April 1728

JACQUES HUBERT BELAIRE—native of Montreal, Canada, son of deceased Ignace Hubert Belaire and Barbe Chauvin and MARGUERITE CATHERINE NEVEU—native of Montreal, Canada, daughter of deceased Jacques Neveu and Michel Chauvin, widow of Etienne Roy. The parties are of second degree of consanguinity.

9 July 1725

CLAUDE HUMBERT called St. Laurent—native of St. Laurent Laroche, diocese of Besancon, son of Christophe Humbert and Marie Ritchay, widower of Marie Anne Le Fort who died in this parish and GILLES THEREZE LE COMTE—native of Paris, parish of St. Nicolas des Champs, daughter of Pierre Le Comte and Marie Bourgeois.

25 February 1723

CLAUDE HUMBIOT—sailor and MARIE ANNE FORT—daughter of Francois Fort, native of Nante on the Seine.

12 May 1725

NICOLAS HUOT—esquire, Seigneur de Vaubery, captain of the Company's ship *Le Dromadaire,* son of deceased Mr. Nicolas Huot, esquire, Seigneur de Vaubery, while living captain of the regiment of the Vielle Marine, and Mlle. Marie Thereze Nicolas des Milets of the parish of St. Nicolas des Chardonnets in Paris and GENEVIEVE TREPANIER—daughter of deceased Sieur Claude Trepanier, while living, an inhabitant of this colony on the lower River St. Louis.

16 June 1721

FRANCOIS HUPE—son of Jean Hupé and Anne Hubert and MARIE ANNE CHARLOTTE—daughter of Jean Charlot and Elizabeth Le Ferre.

16 August 1721

FRANCOIS HUPE—son of Jean Hupé and Jeanne Humbert, of Paris and ANNE LANGE—daughter of Antoine Lange and Marguerite de Beauvais, of the parish of St. Eustache, Paris.

15 November 1728

LAURENT HURLOT—surgeon at Natchez, native of Bas Poitou, bishopric of La Rochelle, son of deceased Tixerant Hurlot and Judith Cuichet and CATHERINE NOTACHE—now of this parish, native of Bayonne, daughter of Jean Notache and Catherine Trouiller.

3 August 1727

JACQUES—Negro, son of Joseph and Marie and MARGUERITE—Negresse. Both belong to Monsieur de Bienville.

THE NEW ORLEANS FRENCH

1 November 1727

Consent of Father Raphael for the marriage of two Negroes, **JACQUES LOUIS** and **LOUISE**, who belong to the Capucin Order.

2 July 1727

LOUIS JAMBOT—native of Montauban, soldier in the Company of Mr. Dustiné, widower of Jeanne Bobas who died in Louisiana and **ELIZA-BETH DELONAY**—native of near Versailles, widow of Louis Beignon.

25 April 1732

JEAN and **CHARLOTTE**. Both parties of Negro slaves belonging to De Bienville, heretofore, Commandant-General of Louisiana.

23 April 1721

RENE JEAN—son of Pierre Jean and René Poirier and **CATHERINE HUBERT**—daughter of Jean Hubert and Barbe Ambroise.

4 June 1727

PIERRE IGNACE JET—son of Jean Germain Jet and Anne Marie Simon, parents living at Bois de Montjean, principality of Polantru (?) and **MARIE ANNE ST. AUBIN**—daughter of Francois St. Aubin, captain at the Invalides and Catherine Durant of the bishopric of Lauanne (?).

4 May 1723

MONSIEUR JACQUES JOLY—master brewer and **MARIE** [Chanio? This name was written in the margin, as though it were the family name instead of:] **MARMOTIER**.

25 May 1733

JOSEPH and **MARIE LOUISE**, Negro slaves belonging to de Bienville, commandant-general of Louisiana.

22 October 1720

Certification of the priest at old Fort Biloxi on the marriage of **FRANCOIS JOTTEUR**—drummer of Mr. Le Blanc's Company and **RENE FREMOND**.

30 April 1730

JACQUES JUDICE—son of Barthelemy Judice and Jeanne Lemaire, native of Thianeour (?), bishopric of Besancon and **MARIE JEANTY**—native of Therée, bishopric of La Rochelle, widow of Antoine Gabinion called Frappe, who died at Natchez.

21 January 1722, Old Biloxi

Certification of the marriage of **JEAN KATCEBERGUE**—native of Idelbert, Germany and **MARIE CHRISTINE**—native of Vicelocq, Germany. Both are workers for the Royal Company of the Indies.

15 July 1733

IVES KERET called Durivage—widower of deceased Jeanne Gourette, native of St. Servais, bishopric of St. Malo, son of deceased Jean Keret and Perine Daniel and **MARIE ALEXIS LE COMTE**—widow of Martin Crié, who died at Natchez, daughter of Francois le Comte and Marie le Loup, native of Luxembourg, archbishopric of Treves.

54

THE NEW ORLEANS FRENCH

5 February 1731

JEAN YVES KERET [Kiret] –son of Ive Keret and Jeanne Guret, native of St. Malo, bishopric of St. Malo and **CLAUDINE PRO**–daughter of Pierre Pro and Jeanne Pellerin, native of Besancon, parish of Ste. Magdelaine, bishopric of Besancon.

5 June 1721

JACQUES KESTON–son of Antoine Keston and Anne [Blank] and **MARIE JEANNE BLEQUOT**–daughter of Charles Blequot and Marie Francois Ducro.

12 January 1728

JACQUES KINDELER–native of Switzerland, son of Christian Kindeler and Magdelaine Rider [or Riden] and **MARGUERITE RIXENER**–daughter of Jean George Rixener and Barbe Selsonbach.

6 December 1728

JACQUES KINDELER–native of Switzerland, son of Christian Kindeler and Magdelaine Roden, widower of Marguerite Kilgeré, who died in Louisiana and **ANNE MARIE CLAUEN** [or Claues ?], native of Durlack in Germany, widow of Daniel Schelle, burger, who died at the German Coast, daughter of Balthazar Clauen and Catherine.

30 June 1726

CONRAD KUGHEL–native of Protad (?), diocese of Spire (?), son of deceased Gregoire Kugel and Anne Marie Wirman, [Ed. note–Although unclear, it is indicated that the father died at L'Orient.] and **ANNE MARGUERITE SCHMID** from Wahenhim (?)–diocese of Maience, daughter of Schmid and Francoise Bouler.

THE NEW ORLEANS FRENCH

3 September 1725

JEAN LABRO—native of Etannen (?), bishopric of Agen, parish of St. Pierre, son of deceased Jean Labro, while living, an officer on the concession of Mr. Lassel (?), and Francoise Bonnefoue and **JEANNE GIL-BERT**—native of the parish of Mobile, daughter of deceased Rene Gilbert and Marguerite Burelle, habitant of this colony, widow of Jean Bacher (?), surgeon.

9 June 1721

SIMON LA CAILLE—son of Francois La Caille and Jeanne Blanpain and **MAGDELAINE MERCIER**—daughter of Jean Baptiste Mercier and Louise Bourgeois.

16 March 1721

FRANCOIS LA FERIERE called Bouillie—son of Francois Bouillie and Marguerite Rousseau and **MARIE FRANCOISE BIENVENU**—daughter of Philipe Bienvenu and Francois Clair.

13 February 1730

JACQUES LA GRANGE called Contant—resident of the lower river, son of Jacques la Grange and Marie Francois, native of Floremuille (?), bishopric of Trem and **ELIZABETH RUELAN** called Nouvellean—daughter of Alin Ruelan and Marguerite Gironet, native of the parish of Tasse (?), bishopric of Cournouailles.

26 February 1725

MR. CLAUDE JOUSSET LA LOIRE—son of deceased Jean Baptist Jousset de la Loire, habitant of Montreal, and Marie Anne Nadot and **MARIE ANNE LE BLANC**—daughter of deceased Henry Le Blanc and Susanne Le Marié.

THE NEW ORLEANS FRENCH

11 August 1721

HONORE LAMBERT—son of Barthelemy Lambert and Catherine Solas and LOUISE BLOIS—daughter of Pierre Blois and Agnes Lucad (??).

12 May 1722

MR. JOSEPH LAMY—son of Mr. Joseph Lamy and Madelaine Marie de [Blank], native of the parish of Sorel in Canada, now of Illinois and MLLE. RICAR—daughter of Mr. Antoine Rivart called La Vigne and Madame Marie Briar of this parish.

5 January 1733

PIERRE FRANCOIS LANCIEN—native of Rouen, parish of St. Goder, bishopric of Rouen in Normandy, son of Jean Lancien, wine merchant, and Marguerite Valtier and JEANNE CAROIX—native of Chaumont in Balligny, parish of St. Martin, diocese of Langres, daughter of Claude, master surgeon, and Jeanne Puillont, widow of Jacques Talmont, who died in Louisiana.

6 June 1730

JEAN BAPTISTE LANIER called Beaupré—native of Orleans, son of Martial Lanier and Catherine Nuland and ELIZABETH LA COMBE—native of La Rochelle, parish of Notre Dame, daughter of Mathieu La Combe and Renée Dusault, widow of Louis Godin, who died at Natchez.

57

16 April 1730

JEAN BAPTISTE LAPIERRE—soldier in the Company of Dustiné, native of Frenois in Champagne, bishopric of Langres, son of Charles Lapierre and Anne Carteret, widower of Toussaint Pignon, who died at Biloxi and **MARIE BELIARD**—native of Jalay, diocese of Angers, daughter of Louis Belliard and Michel Durand, widow of Francois Dinier (?), who died in Louisiana.

28 November 1724

JEAN BAPTISTE LAPRADE—native of Chateau Riché, diocese of Quebec, major son of Jean Baptiste Laprade and Marie Magdelaine Cloutier of the same place and **ELIZABETH SIMON**—native of the parish of St. Jean de La Rochelle, daughter of Joseph Simon, native of Quebec, and Marie Foucault. Note: Signed by f.f. Caston, "religieux aumonier" of the *Profond*, because there was "aumonier" here nor at Fort Louis Le Biloxi. Signed at the habitation of Lapointe St. Joseph, Riviere des Paskagoulas, province of Louisiana.

21 October 1725 (Renewal of vows)

JEAN BAPTISTE LAPRADE—native of the parish of Chateau Richer, diocese of Quebec, son of Jean Baptiste Laprade, and Marie Magdelaine Cloutier of the same place and **ELIZABETH SIMON**—native of St. Jean de la Rochelle, daughter of Joseph Simon, native of Quebec, now inhabitant of this colony, and Marie Franquou. [Married 8 November 1724]

5 February 1721, Old Biloxi

JACQUES LARCHEVEQUE—son of Jean Larcheveque and Catherine Delounay of Canada, parish of Notre Dame in Quebec and **MARIE LEMOINE.**

THE NEW ORLEANS FRENCH

4 December 1730

FRANCOIS LARCHEVESQUE—son of Jean Larchevesque and Marie Magdelaine, native of Quebec and **JULIENNE LA BROSSE**—daughter of Gille la Brosse and Jeanne Poussin, native of Rhemmes in Brittany. Joseph Larchevesque is the groom's brother.

7 November 1729

JOSEPH LARCHEVESQUE—resident on the upper river, son of Jean Larchevesque and Catherine Delonay, native of "que d'une part" (*sic*) and **MARGUERITE FRANCOISE LE COQ**—daughter of Francois Le Coq and Suzanne Demons, native of Havre de Grace, parish of St. Germain.

25 June 1733

FRANCOIS LA ROCHE—native of Montreal in Canada, son of deceased Jean La Roche and Magdelaine L'Heureuse and **FRANCOISE LUCE**—native of Dunquerque in Flanders, daughter of deceased Pierre Luce and Marie Jeanne Dubois.

5 July 1730

PIERRE LA ROCHE—master carpenter, son of Pierre La Roche and Marie Vilain, native of Clermont in Auvergne, parish of St. Hilaire, widower of Marie Elexis, who died at Mobile and **MARIE DAUDIN**—daughter of Charles Daudin and Marie Guerin, native of Orleans, parish of St. Victor [or Victoir], widow of Antoine Michel Caron, "patron" of the Company, who died at Natchez.

59

THE NEW ORLEANS FRENCH

13 June 1730

NICOLAS JOSEPH LARQUAIS—native of Rheims in Champagne, son of Pierre Larquais and Nicole Chatelin and CATHERINE ELIZABETH LE BLANC—daughter of André Le Blanc and Catherine Renard, native of Chouat in Saxe, widow of Nicolas Alexandre, who died at Natchez.

1 November 1728

PIERRE SEBASTIEN LARTAUD—master tailor, native of La Rochelle, parish of Notre Dame, son of Pierre Lartaud, also master tailor, and Catherine Roy, widower of Louise Benedict le Fel [or Bel], who died in Louisiana and MARIE ROUSSEAU—native of St. Jean d'Angelique, bishopric of Saintes, daughter of Francois Rousseau and Marie Anne Perrault, widow of George Vomier, who died in Louisiana.

28 April 1721

PIERRE SEBASTIEN LARTEAU—son of Pierre L'Artau and Catherine Roan and LOUISE BENEDIE LESEL [or Lefel] —daughter of Mathieu Lefel and Marie Laporte.

16 July 1726

JOSEPH LASSUS—native of Mareilly (?), bishopric of Comminge (?), son of Jean Antoine de Lassus and Jeanne La Forgne and GENEVIEVE BUREL—widow of Claudetre Panier (?), who died in Louisiana.

5 October 1723

PIERRE LAURENT—Soldier in the Company of Sieur Barnaval at Natchitoches, native of Fougeres in Brittany, parish of St. Leonnard and ISABELLE DUBAN—daughter of René Duban, worker in the Company of the Indies at New Orleans, and deceased Isabelle Duval.

THE NEW ORLEANS FRENCH

3 September 1720

JEAN LA VERGNE—native of Chatellerau, son of deceased Pierre La Vergne and Francois Simon and **FRANCOISE FLASSIN**—native of Versaille, daughter of deceased Pierre Flassin and Barbe Ioux (?).

4 July 1725

LOUIS LA VERGNE—native of Quebec, now inhabitant of Paskagoula River, son of Louis La Vergne and Marie Simon, bourgeois of Quebec and **ELIZABETH THOMMELIN**—daughter of Pierre Tommelin, *menuissier* of this town, and deceased Marguerite Coussenote.

5 June 1729

HENRY LA VILLE—native of Dazé le Rideau, bishopric of Tour, son of deceased Jean Laville and Louise Rossard, soldier in the Company of Mr. de Gavry (?), widower of M - - - (?), who died at Biloxi and **ANNE MARIE MULER**—native of Souabe, daughter of deceased Joseph Muler and Barbe.

5 October 1728

HENRY LEBEL—native of Paris, son of Pierre Lebel and Bastienne Benard and **ANNE MARIE LANDRY**—native of Basel in Switzerland, daughter of Jacob Landry and A M A [Ed. note—Only these letters were given in the original.]

23 June 1727

PIERRE LE CLERC—native of Cornier in Henau, diocese of Cambray, widower of Marie d'Estendre (?) and **MARIE CHAGNEAU**—native of the Isle de Moutin (?), widow of Jacques Joly, guardian of the storehouse at the Chaumont Concession in Louisiana, daughter of Philibert Chagneaux and Catherine Billard of the bishopric of Lucon in Poitou.

61

THE NEW ORLEANS FRENCH

26 August 1720

FRANCOIS LE COMTE—native of Ypres in Flanders, son of Augustin Le Comte, major surgeon of the city, and Louise du Chatellier and **MAGDELAINE CHAIGNAU**—native of La Rochelle, parish of Notre Dame, daughter of Etienne Chaigneau and Marie Rondelle.

21 July 1721

PHILIPPE JACQUE LE DUC—native of Meney in Flanders and **MARIE ANNE THEREZE MASSON**—native of Mons in Henaux, of the Le Blanc Concession.

30 October 1720, Old Fort Biloxi

MICHEL LE GRAND—native of the parish of St. Mathieu, town of Kimper in Basse Bretagne and **CATHERINE LEQUEDEZ**—native of the same place.

12 March 1725

PIERRE LEHOUX—son of Francois Lehoux and Anne Ruicam of La Rochelle and **MARGUERITE L'ARMUSEAU**—daughter of deceased Jean Baptiste L'Armuseaux, surgeon, and Catherine Esternay.

16 January 1725

ADRIEN LE JAY—native of Senlis (?), son of Antoine Le Jai and Marguerite Perrot, now resident of Natchitoches and **MARIE ANNE LIN-COURT**—native of Francfort, daughter of Joseph Sadalev (?) Lincourt [or Tincourt], and Marie Rose [Blank].

THE NEW ORLEANS FRENCH

8 November 1728

FRANCOIS LE MELLE called Bellegarde—native of Paris, parish of St. Sulpice, son of Francois Lemesle and Marie Coquelin and **MARIE LOUISE MARIETTE**—native of Trene [or Frene] in Germany, daughter of deceased Louis, surgeon-major, and Marguerite. Both parties are now of this parish.

8 August 1720

GILLES LE MIRRE—native of the bourg of La Trenay in Bretagne, diocese of Remmes, son of deceased Guillaume Le Mirre and Perrine Le Roy and **MARIE LOUISE BRUNET**—native of Paris, daughter of Phatio (?) de Montfuin (?) Brunet and Marie Francois. (*sic*)

1 July 1727

CHARLES FRANCOIS LE MOINE—son of Philipe Ignace le Moine of L'Isle in Flanders, bishopric of Tournay [or Lournay], and Marie Marguerite and **ELIZABETH MERCIER**—daughter of Laurent Mercier and Marie Anne Grillet de Macon.

4 April 1725

GUILLAUME LEMOINE—*patron* of a chaloupe of the Company, son of Jacques Le Moine, navigator, and Jeanne _____ , of Havre de Grace, parish of Notre Dame and **MARIE SAUMERINE**—daughter of Elmael Saumerine and Anne Marie Edelme, native of the Palatinat.

23 April 1721

JEAN FRANCOIS LENCLOS (?) DE GALLAIS—son of Jean Francois Lenclos de Gallais and Jeanne Morgau and **MARIE THERESE NEUVILLE**—daughter of Sieur de Neuville and Demoiselle de Breboeuf.

11 July 1730

JEAN BAPTISTE LEONARD—native of Leige, parish of St. Severin, widower of Marie Paulus, who died in Louisiana and **ANNE COUDRAY** —native of Plouanne [or Plonanne], bishopric of St. Malo, daughter of Francois Coudray and Gillet Gautier, widow of Julien Chartier, who died at Natchez.

20 March 1728

LOUIS LEONARD—native of Alexe (?), bishopric of Languedoc, silkworker and resident of Arkansas, son of Jean Leonard and Louise Calais and **MARGUERITE KISTENMACHER**—daughter of Etienne Kistenmacher, resident of the German Coast, and Anne Doware [or Dorvare].

23 April 1721

NICOLAS LE PREUX [or Le Pieux] called Montreuil—son of Claude Le Preu and Jeanne Oudar and **CATHERINE BADI**—daughter of Brie Bady and Louise Arbour.

5 January 1733

PIERRE LE ROY called Feran—native of Paris, son of Pierre and Marie Deslesme and **CLAUDINE GRISON**—native of St. Donat in Dauphiné, bishopric of Vienne, widow of Pierre Renaudot called Sans Chagrin, who died in Louisiana.

12 April 1730

[Ed. note—This record is garbled; it is given here as it appeared in the original.]
PIERRE LE SAGE and Elizabeth Callerien, his mother and father and MARIE FRANCOISE BLEE—native of Paris, parish of St. Paul, daughter of Jean Baptiste Blee and Marie Thereze Marcancour, widow of Louis Pousset, who died at Natchez.

1725 [no other date, but following 6 June and preceding 4 July]

JEAN THOMAS LESCH—inhabitant of this parish, native of Heisdlberg, son of Andre Leich and Anne Gertrude and ANNE SCHODERBECKEN —native of the bishopric of Virtemberg, daughter of deceased Jean George and Anne _____.

25 June 1721

CHARLES LETIENIER (?)—son of Marin Letienier and Barbe Goulet and MARIE FRANCOISE MAGUET—daughter of Jacques Maguet and Marie Cochois (?) [or Cochoin ?] .

16 December 1727

ANTOINE JOSEPH LE VEUF—son of Antoine Le Veuf and Francoise Soupé, widower of Jeanne Damas, who died in Louisiana and CATHERINE RENEE BOIDELO [or Bordelon] —native of the village of Fou, bishopric of Cornouailles, daughter of Augustin Jacques Bordelo (?) and Marguerite Francoise Boisterre (??).

THE NEW ORLEANS FRENCH

12 May 1727

FRANCOIS LINEREUX–soldier of the Company of Dutisné, native of Clermont in Picardy, bishopric of Beauvais, son of Francois Linereux and Anne Soigné and **MARIE TELLIER**–native of Paris, parish of St. Sauveur, daughter of Louis Tellier and Catherine Le Conte.

4 June 1721

PIERRE LIREL–son of Gilles Lirel and Marie Cornine and **LOUISE THERESE L'EVEILLE**–daughter of Jacques L'Eveillé and Marie Magdelaine du Meu.

11 November 1732

MONSIEUR GUILLAUME LOCQUET, Sieur de la Pommeray–Treasurer of the Marine, native of St. Malo De L'Isle, widower of Demoiselle Anne Marie Garnier, who died at St. Malo and **ANNE CATHERINE TRUDEAU**–native of Dauphin Island, widow of Mr. G - - - - de la Boulay, officer of the infantry who died in Louisiana.

29 November 1728

PIERRE PAUL LOISEL–master locksmith, native of St. Jacques de Elison (*sic*), bishopric of Nantes, son of Martin Loisel and deceased Magdelaine Perette and **MARIE CATHERINE BOQUER**–native of Flanders, bishopric of Ypres, daughter of deceased Jean Baptiste Bouquer and Jeanne Piel.

30 June 1721

JOSEPH LOTIERE–native of Philippeville in Henos and **JEANNE DERMUZEAU** [or Desmuzeau] –native of Aueunne (??) in Henos. [Both parties are on the Diron concession.]

66

THE NEW ORLEANS FRENCH

1 November 1721

LOUIS—Negro slave belonging to Mr. Croustilhad and **CATHERINE**—Negro slave belonging to Mr. Croustilhad.

4 April 1728

Consent given by the Director of the Company of the Indies for the marriage of two of their slaves:
LOUIS—Negro from the Congo, "maitre des hautes ouevres," and **SUZANNE**—Negresse.

9 April 1731

ETIENNE LOUIS—native of Orleans, parish of St. Nicolas, son of Charles Louis and Jeanne Deletee and **ANNE FOUCHEUR**—native of La Chapelle, widow of Louis Henry, who died at Natchez.

4 March 1721, Old Biloxi

ANTOINE LOVE—son of Daniel Love and Marie Butter (?) and **MARIE ANNE JOMAR**—daughter of Jean Jomar and Marie Claude Douar.

24 April 1726

JOSEPH LUZON—son of Joseph Lazon [or Lazou] and Catherine Cham (?), captain of the *traversie* L'Abeitte, in the service of the Company of the Indies and **MARIE LOUISE BALIVET**—widow of Jacques Duval, who died in the sinking of a ship [or boat].

30 June 1727

PHILIPE JACQUES LYAN or Tyan or Tzan—widower of Marguerite Wichthenen who died at the German Coast and **ANNE MARIE SCHLATTER BECKEN**—native of the duchy of Vitemberg, widow of Jacob Stalle who died at the German Coast.

17 June 1721

BARTHELEMY MADRE—son of Pierre Madré and Jeanne Jolicoeur and **FRANCOISE SAVARY**—daughter of Jean Baptiste Savary and Louise Francoise Langlois.

11 (or 17) August 1720

ETIENNE MAJARDON—son of Louis Maiardon and Marie La Roche, native of Libourne, diocese of Bordeaux and **MARIE MARGUERITE GREVE**—daughter of Jacques Grevé and Marie Lieffre (?) Hodoud (?), native of Villeneuve le Roy in Bourgogne, diocese of Sem (?).

1 May 1727

JEAN ANTOINE MALON—native of Turin, son of Francois Malon and Anne Marie and **MARIE MAGDELAINE MANGON DE LA TOUR**—native of Aras, daughter of Mathieu Mangon de la Tour and Marie Magdelaine Lejont.

5 May 1732

FRANCOIS MANARD—native of Marsienne sur Lesearpe (?), bishopric of Aras, drummer in the company of Mr. Renault Dautrive, heretofore married to Anne Sybille, who died in Louisiana and **MARIE PARIS**—native of Orleans, widow of Antoine Joblin [or Jablin] called Sans Louis [St. Louis ?], who died in Louisiana.

THE NEW ORLEANS FRENCH

23 April 1726

JEAN FRANCOIS MANNARD—resident of New Orleans, widower of Marie Catherine Manera, who died in Louisiana and ANNE MARIE SIBILLE—widow of Jacques Henry Bourgeois, who died in Louisiana.

31 July 1721

PIERRE MARCHAND and MARIE CATHERINE VERDEVERREST (?).

1 April 1721

CLAUDE PIERRE MARESCHAL called Villeneuvre—son of Jean Mareschal and Catherine Chapin and MARIE ANNE GONO called Rose —daughter of Pierre Gono and Marie Rose.

26 June 1730

JEAN MARET, esquire—officer of the troops in this colony, native of La Rochefoucault, diocese of Angouleme, son of Charles Maret, esquire, and Marie Juzat and MARIE LOIGGET—native of St. Malo, daughter of Jean Baptiste Loigget and Marie le Jaloux.

6 May 1730

CHARLES MARQUET—master sail-maker, native of Medriad, bishopric of St. Malo, son of Julien Marquet and Fleury Nanté, widower of Jeanne Legrand, who died at Hanssiat [or Haussiat] and MARIE ROSE DOREE [or Dorié]—daughter of Jean Baptiste D - - - and Francoise Chartin, native of Port Louise, widow of Francois Carlo, who died at Natchez.

69

30 June 1725

ANTOINE MARTIN—*Indien* of the Apalache nation and **JEANNE**, *Indienne* of Black River.

12 October 1723

RODOFFE MARTIN—native of Switzerland and **MARGUERITE BES-SOTE**—widow of Gregoire Schein [or Schem] .

9 January 1726

PIERRE MARTINOT—native of Beauvais in Brie, archbishopric of Sens, habitant of this parish and **MARIE JOLY**—native of Chateau Gontier, bishopric of Angers. [The marriage was actually celebrated at Biloxi 18 September 1721.]

15 November 1728

GABRIEL MASSIAUX—native of La Rochelle, parish of Notre Dame, resident of Natchez, son of deceased Pierre Massiaux and Dame Fournier and **LUCE CRETHE**—native of Neufchalet in Switzerland, daughter of Jaam Crethe and Jeanne Creune (?).

4 September 1731

JEAN BAPTISTE MASSY—sindic at New Orleans, native of Tours in Tourraine, son of Jean Baptiste Massy, bourgeois of that town, and Catherine Rufray [or Rufran] and **JEANNE FANCON DU MANOIR**—native of St. Malo, daughter of Jean Baptiste du Manoir, heretofore, Director of the Concession of St. Catherine, and Charlotte le Jaloux.

THE NEW ORLEANS FRENCH

14 June 1729

JEAN LOUIS MATE—master carpenter, native of Neufchatel in Switzerland, canton of Berne, son of Jean Louis Maté and Anne Cherbillye and **FRANCOISE ARBERT**—native of St. Donat in Dauphiné, widow of Gaspart Didier, master joiner, who died in Louisiana.

6 July 1730

ETIENNE MATEE—native of Coublanc, bishopric of Langres, son of Etienne Matée and Jeanne Theriot and **MARIE MARTIN**—native of Languedoc, daughter of Sebastien Martin and Dame Demeron, widow of Pierre Lambremon, who died at Natchez.

18 October 1723

LAURENT MAYET—native of Paris, shoemaker and **ANNE THEREZE GARNY** [or Garsy] **d'OSTENDE**—native of the parish of Notre Dame. Note: The place of birth may be Ostende, parish of Notre Dame.

19 March 1722

Declaration that Father Maximim on ascending to Natchez, married **GASPARD MAZAVOT** and **GENEVIEVE GOYER**.

26 April 1728

LOUIS MENAGER—native of Paris, parish of St. Paul, son of deceased Jean Baptiste Menager, *menuisier* and Marguerite _____ and **ANNE THEREZE PERDUIEL** (?)—native of Paris, daughter of Jean Perdriel and Thereze Charlotte Labouré, widow of Jean Simonet, who died in Louisiana.

71

THE NEW ORLEANS FRENCH

25 July 1730

PIERRE MENIE—native of Rheimes in Brittany, son of Francois Menie and Jeanne Pelerbe and **CATHERINE ANHAT** [or Auhat] —native of Makal in Saxe, widow of Jean Charles Camberlet, who died at Natchez.

30 December 1726

JEAN FREDERIC MERQUELE—native of Kalssenveuten (?), in the duchy of Wirtemburg, son of Jean Leonnard Merquelé and Marguerite Hirlé, widower of Anne Marie Kolheiffen, who died in the German Coast and **ANNE BARBE FREDERIC**—daughter of Conrad Frederic and Ursule Freyer. Both are residents of the German Coast.

8 May 1721

MICHEL MERUAN—son of Michel Meruan and Louise [Blank] and **MARIE LOUISE LE ROY**—daughter of Louis Le Roy and Marie Renard.

23 February 1722

ALEXANDRE METUNIER (?)—son of Jacques Metunier and Perine Lamo and **PERETTE VOLIER**—daughter of Nicolas Volier and Genevieve Belcour, widow of Alexandre Nicolas Capel.

21 January 1726

JEAN MICHAUX called Meunier—son of Pierre Michaux and Marguerite Bironne, soldier in the garrison at Natchitoches, native of Deprez in Poitou, bishopric of Lucon and **NICOLLE VIELLE VIELLE** (*sic*)—daughter of deceased Francois Vielle Vielle and Marguerite Gaille.

72

THE NEW ORLEANS FRENCH

24 November 1726

ROCH MICHEL—employee of the Company of the Indies, native of Paris, parish of St. Sulpice, faubourg St. Germain, son of Francois Jacques Michel de Liege [or from Liege], and Jeanne Flaneau (?) and **LOUISE PHILIPPEAUX**—daughter of André Philippeau, master turner, native of Maran, bishopric of La Rochelle, and Elizabeth Boureau, widow of Noel Le Fevre, who was a baker in New Orleans.

16 May 1730

RENE ANTOINE MILLET—son of Antoine Millet and Marie Jeanne Elizabeth Motel, native of Paris, parish of St. Roch and **MARIE TOUT-DIT**—daughter of Francois Toutdit and Suzanne Glenard, native of Vannes in Brittany "paroisse Dumenez."

27 November 1727

JEAN MINGO—Free Negro, who states that he well knows the servile condition of the bride and **THEREZE**—negresse slave of the Castillon Concession. In the presence of Darby, director of the concession.

29 June 1729

JEAN BAPTISTE MONTARD—master joiner, native of Paris, parish of St. Sulpice, son of Jean Montard, master joiner of Paris, and Marie Jeanne Pin and **MARIE MONTFREIN** called Brunet—native of Paris, parish of St. André, daughter of deceased Felix de Montfrein and Marie Brunet, widow of Gilles Lemine [or Lemire] called Le Breton, who died in Louisiana.

73

THE NEW ORLEANS FRENCH

4 June 1729

JOSEPH MOREAU—master locksmith, widower of Jeanne Lamourette, who died in Louisiana and **THEREZE LEGRAND**—native of Beville (?) en Mere (Belle Isle en Mer ?), bishopric of Vannes, widow of Pierre Drillant, who died in Louisiana.

28 May 1725, Balize Island

JEAN PIERRE MOREL—*menuissier*, son of Pierre Morel, master menuissier in Paris, parish of St. Nicolas du Chardonnet, and Rene Baudin and **MARIE MARGUERITE ANGRAND** [or Augrand]—widow of Robert Blanquette, daughter of Michel Angrand, master mason at Dieppe, parish of St. Remy, bishopric of Rhouan, and Elizabeth Alard.

17 May 1728

PAUL ANTOINE MULER—native of Hale in Saxe, son of Cristoffe Muler and Marguerite Quindreman and **MARIE FRANCOISE BOUR-DON**—daughter of Francois Bourdon and Claudine de la Haye, residents of New Orleans.

28 April 1727

DAVID MUNIER—native of La Neuville, bishopric of Bale (?) in Switzerland, son of Etienne Munier and Marguerite Grosjean, carpenter in the service of the Company of the Indies and **MARIE ELIZABETH KERNER**—native of Palatinat, widow of Jean George Kretzer, who died here.

THE NEW ORLEANS FRENCH

19 April 1729

DAVID MUNIER—carpenter, native of Darberg, canton of Berne in Switzerland, son of deceased Etienne Munier and Marguerite Grosjean, widower of Elizabeth Kerner (?), who died in Louisiana and **MARIE ANNE VERNE**—native of Kolmar in Alsace, daughter of Jacques Verné and Marie Anne Jean.

19 April 1730

MARTIN MUNIER—native of Cobré, "pais de Hainau," archbishopric of Cambray, son of Lugues (?) Munier and Marie Jeanne Houdar and **LOUISE TANTIBOTE**—native of L'Orient, bishopric of Vannes, daughter of Jean Tibotte (*sic*) and Marie Fraualle, widow of Jean Louis Langueville, who died at Natchez.

12 February 1725

LUC MARTIN NANTIER—joiner, native of Soisson, habitant of Chapitoulas and **MARIE THEREZE LETIER**—native of Aras, widow of Demaret.

21 August 1728

MARTIN NANTIER called Soisson—native of Soisson in Picardy, son of Sulpice Nantier and deceased Marguerite Moreau, widower of Therese Lattiere, who died in Louisiana and **ADRIENNE AUMARE**—native of Neuilly (?) St. Frond, bishopric of Soissons, daughter of Louis Aumare and deceased Elizabeth Callin, widow of Louis Bodin of Pointe Coupee, who died there.

THE NEW ORLEANS FRENCH

10 January 1731

JEAN NAVERE—son of Bernard Navere and Jeanne Larode, native of St. Nicolas of the town of Plaisance, bishopric of Larbe (?) in Gascony, widower of Louise Bridon, who died in Louisiana and **THERESE MISO-NET**—daughter of Antoine Misonet and Magdelaine Malbé, native of the parish of St. Nicolas des Champs in Paris, archbishopric of Paris, widow of Louis Miraut, who died at Natchez. The act was signed: Therese Maisonaite and Jean Naveres.

4 June 1721

ANTOINE NEGRIER—son of Francois Negrier and Marie Burelle and **MARGUERITE BEGUINE**—daughter of Jean Baptiste Beguiné and Marguerite Souverene.

29 December 1725

NICOLAS NOISET—native of Noirval, diocese of Rheims, son of deceased Jean Noiset and Elizabeth Renaud, habitant of the said Noirval and **CATHERINE BARBE**—native of Colmar, bishopric of Strasbourg, daughter of Nicolas Barbe and Elizabeth N. (*sic*).

27 August 1726

PIERRE OLIVAUX—native of Champagne, diocese of La Rochelle, son of deceased Laurent Olivaux and Helene Robert and **MARIE MAGDE-LAINE GAFFEL**—daughter of deceased Leonard Gaffel and Catherine Volf, who is now the wife, in second marriage, of André Schantz of Germany [or possibly the German Coast].

76

THE NEW ORLEANS FRENCH

10 November 1727

JACQUES OZENNE—Wet cooper for the Company, native of St. Loo in Basse Normandy, son of deceased Philippe Ozenne and Marthe Dumoulin and **CHARLOTTE MOREAU**—daughter of Joseph Moreau, locksmith, and deceased Jeanne Dummourette [or Dammourette].

30 October 1730

FRANCOIS ELOY PARIS called St. Francois—son of Francois Paris, native of Versailles and **BARBE COLIN**—native of the bishopric of Cornouailles, daughter of Jean Colin and Jeanne Vannerek (?).

16 June 1727

DANIEL PAUL [other records indicate that this should be Boff] —native of Cassen, diocese of Spire, widower of Marie Eve Kaume [Kaime ?], who died in Louisiana and **ANNE MARIE WERICH**—native of "Lampailz Loraine Almande," diocese of Metz, daughter of deceased Nicolas Werich and Anne Marie. Neither party knew how to sign their names.

24 March 1729

GERAD PELLERIN—guardian of the storehouse, churchwarden of the parish of New Orleans, son of Robert Pellerin and Elizabeth Foulon, native of Mezieres sur Meme, bishopric of Remmes, widower of Angelique Catherine Lecoise (?), who died in Louisiana and **FRANCOISE RUELAN**—daughter of Pierre Ruelan and Francoise Henon, of the parish of Pleneuf, diocese of St. Brien, widow of Jean Baptist Scolan, notary and agent in the jurisdiction of St. Malo.

1 September 1722

PIERRE PELOIN–son of Louis Peloin and Catherine Razard and **MARIE FORT LE ROY**–daughter of Pierre Le Roy and Jeanne La Porte.

24 May 1728

FRANCOIS PENTURAUX–native of St. Maelon [or Maclon], bishopric of Poitiers, son of deceased Benoist Penturaux and Anne Metayer and **MARIE ANNE BAUREGARD**–native of Nantes in Brittany, parish of St. Nicolas, daughter of deceased Pierre Bauregard and Marie Jeanne Philbert, widow of Pierre Eurard, wheelright.

6 August 1726

RENE PERIE–Mareschal Ferand of the Company of the Indies, native of Port Louis, widow of Marie Anne Gots, who died in Louisiana and **LOUISE GALAIS**–widow of Louis La Fond, voyager who died in this parish, native of St. B - - negue (?), bishopric of Cornouailles.

13 June 1730

JACQUES PERIER–native of the archbishopric of Rouen, son of Jacques Perier and Marguerite _____ and **GABRIELLE TRUITTE**– daughter of Etienne Truitte and Anne Blauché [or Blanché], widow of Gilles Avotte (?), who died in Louisiana.

THE NEW ORLEANS FRENCH

22 November 1728

JOSEPH PETIT—resident of New Orleans, native of St. Paul de Loen, bishopric of St. Paul, parish of St. Jean, son of Paul Petit and Marie Palu, widower of Marie Jeanne Chevalier, who died in Louisiana and **FRANCOISE LE SEURE**—native of Nantes in Brittany, daughter of Jacques Le Seure and Francoise Auguet, widow of Louis Bonnaventure, who died in Louisiana.

26 February 1731

LOUIS PETIT COULONGE LIVILLIERS—son of deceased Charles Petit Livilliers, esquire, captain of the infantry, and Magdelaine Gautier de Varonne, native of Montreal and **FRANCOISE GALARD**—native of L'Isle Dauphine, daughter of Francois Galard and Marie Anne Evrieux (?).

14 January 1726

CHARLES PETIT DE LIVILLIER—esquire, seigneur de Livillier in Picardy, son of Charles Claude Petit de Coulange, esquire, seigneur de Livillier, captain of the Marine, and Marie Gauthier de la Verendrie and **ESTIENNETTE LOUISE MALBEQUE**—native of Brest, daughter of Jean Malbeq, commissioner of stores for the Marine, and Thomas Anne Le Cler. [Among the witnesses were Mr. De Verteuil, *beaufrere* of the bride, and Mdme. De Verteuil, the bride's sister.]

24 March 1721

PIERRE PICHON—native of Lyon, parish of St. Vincent, son of Antoine Picon (?) of Switzerland and Marie Anne Guillemot of Cambray in Flanders and **MARIE JEANNE LONGUEVILLE**—native of Faubourg St. Jacques. Both parties are living on the Mississippi River.

THE NEW ORLEANS FRENCH

10 May 1726

PIERRE PICHON—native of Lion, parish of St. Vincent, son of Antoine Pichon and Marie Anne Guilman, soldier at Natchitoches and **CATHERINE LUCA**, native of L'Orient, bishopric of Vannes, daughter of Guillaume Luca and Marie Mellie.

21 July 1733

URBAIN PICOU—son of deceased Charles Picou and Jeanne Pouppon, native of Brest, bishopric of St. Paul and **MARIE JOSEPH LARMUISSAU**—daughter of deceased Thomas Larmuissau and Catherine Favre, native of Auverne (?) in Hainau.

24 May 1733

PIERRE and **JEANNETON**, Negro slaves belonging to the Capuchin Order.

18 April 1730

NICOLAS PIERRON—resident of New Orleans, native of the bishopric of Chalon sur Mane, son of Claude Pierron and Elizabeth La Roze and **MAGDELAINE L'ESVESQUE**—native of La Rochelle, daughter of deceased Sulpice L'Evesque and Magdelaine Prez, widow of Gabriel Poulain, who died at Natchez.

9 June 1721

MAURICE PIGNY—son of Louis Pigny and Marguerite Anne Sacequepée (?) and **MARGUERITE LETELLIER** called Margot Denis—daughter of Francois Letellier and Catherine Lauernier.

THE NEW ORLEANS FRENCH

25 June 1722

JEAN EMOND PITACHE—son of Mr. Francois Pitache and Marie Malacot and **CATHERINE PIE**—daughter of Guillaume Pied and Marie Le Danois, widow of Francois [Blank].

19 October 1718, Dauphine Island

PIERRE PITARD—son of Jean Pitard and Anne Paris and **LOUISE MARTHE SEGUIN**—daughter of Claude Seguin and Marthe Gé. This is a certification by Father Raphael of a marriage performed by Father Le Maire, priest of the foreign missions. Certified 17 November 1727.

3 April 1721

LUCIEN POIRE—native of Paris, parish of St. Eustache, son of Lucien Poiré and Catherine Luead (?) and **MARGUERITE TOULOUZE** [or Loulouze] —daughter of Claude Toulouze and Louise. The bride states that she does not know her mother's last name. She is a native of the parish of St. Fermin in Picardy.

7 May 1721

JEAN FRANCOIS POMEL—son of Pierre Pomel and Marie Jeanne Chardru and **CATHERINE GONZALOU**—daughter of Jean Baptiste Gonzalau and Catherine Viellemain.

3 February 1722

NICOLAS PORTIER called Joly—son of Enry Portier and Elizabeth Vautran and **MAGDELAINE POMON** [or Ponson] —daughter of Pierre Pomon [or Ponson] and Marguerite Peltier.

81

18 November 1726

JEAN GABRIEL POULAIN—resident of Natchez, widower of Marie Godilonne [or Jodilonne], who died at Natchez, native of Paris, parish of St. Roch, son of Claude Poulain, master sculptor, and Jeanne Turpin and **MAGDELAINE MARGUERITE L'EVESQUE**—daughter of Sulpice L'Evesque, master locksmith of New Orleans, and Magdelaine Prez.

17 May 1728

EDME POUPART—native of Paris, parish of St. Sulpice, son of deceased Pierre Poupart and Catherine Cantty [or Cautty] and **ANNE MARIE FREDERICK**—native of the German Coast, daughter of Jean Conrad Frederick and Ursule Krenter (?).

19 February 1722, Fort Louis

ETIENNE POUSSARD—son of Nicolas Poussard and Jeanne Laurens, native of the parish of Boncour, bishopric of Chartres in Beauce and **ETIENETTE VAUCEL**—daughter of Julien Vaucel and Perine Gymard, native of the town of Rhennes in Bretagne, parish of La Toussain.

22 May 1730

JEAN PRADEL—infantry captain, native of Perche in Limousin, parish of Notre Dame, son of deceased Jacques Pradel de Lamaze, lieutenant-general at the siege of Zerche, and Gille de Maledan and **ALEXAN-DRINE DE LA CHAISE**—native of Nantes in Brittany, daughter of deceased Mr. de la Chaise, Commissioner of the King, and Marguerite Cailly.

THE NEW ORLEANS FRENCH

9 May 1729

MR. LOUIS PRAT—King's doctor and Councilor on the Superior Council of Louisiana, son of Jean Prat, bourgeois of the town of La Guilole, diocese of Rhodes, and Anne Sattel (?) and **MARIE LOUISE DE LA CHAISE**—eldest daughter of Mr. de la Chaise, King's Commissioner and First Councilor, and Marguerite Cailly.

18 June 1732

NICOLAS PREVOST—native of Longuille, bishopric of Boulogne, son of Claude Prevost and Marie Rornie (??) and **MARIE THERESE BERTRAND**—daughter of Pierre Bertrand and Francoise Poupon, native of Brest, parish of St. Sauveur, bishopric of St. Paul de Lion.

5 April 1723

NICOLAS PROVET—carpenter and **JACQUETTE MAISONNEUF**—native of Breste.

15 July 1721

NICOLAS PROVET and **FRANCOISE ROUSSET** [Both parties are of the Concession of the Marquis d'ArKeny ?]

12 January 1733

JEAN BAPTISTE RABALAY—resident of Pointe Coupée, native of Rochefoucant in Poitou, son of Jean Baptiste Rabalay and Marie Magdelaine and **MARGUERITE BELLANGER**—native of Suire (?), archbishopric of Paris, widow of Joseph Ducro, who died at Natchez.

THE NEW ORLEANS FRENCH

13 April 1733

EDME FRANCOIS RACLOT—native of Idigny, diocese of Sens, parish of St. Thibault, son of Edmé Raclot and Marguerite Sommier [or Lommier] and **GABRIELLE MORAN**—native of Orange, widow of Francois Fortié, resident of New Orleans, died on the ship *La Gironde*.

23 November 1726

DANIEL RAFFLAND—*coureur*, native of Bel, canton of Berne, son of Jean Raffland and Marie Wittebach, widower of Anne Barbe Kupfler (?), who died at La Baine (?) and **MARIE MARGUERITE BEZEL**—daughter of Louis Bezel and Anne Marguerite, from Neustadt in the marquisat of Bareth, widow of Rodolph Martin, who died in Louisiana.

4 May 1728

JEAN BAPTISTE CLAUDE RAGUET—native of Tours in Touraine, formerly Procurer for the King in Louisiana, son of Claude Raguet and Jeanne Le Francois, widower of Marie La Rieux, who died in Louisiana and **JEANNE ANNE CORBIN DE LA TOUCHE**—daughter of Jean Marie Corbin de Baschemin and Dame Judith Lehardy, Concessioner on the St. Louis River, native of St. Malo.

29 October 1720, Old Fort Biloxi

PIERRE RAME—sailor, native of the Isle of Oléron and **RENE DURAND**—native of Angers in A₁ᵢou.

THE NEW ORLEANS FRENCH

3 December 1725

JEAN RANDON—native of Bessé in Forest, diocese of Vienne in Dauphiné, son of Jean Randon and Benoite Bilin [or Belin], of this parish and CATHERINE FENERONE—widow of deceased Jean Fabien, while living, a soldier of this garrison, native of Farlouis [or Sarlouis] diocese of Troies, daughter of Francois Fenerone and Anne Marie Sare [or Fare], also of this parish.

1730 [Ed. note—No specific date, but appearing directly
after 30 April]

RAPHAEL—Free Negro and MARIE MAGDELAINE called Fanchon—Negro slave of Mr. Mondonlies (?).

and on the same record:

JEAN BAPTISTE MACHINY—Negro slave of Mr. Perrier and BABE.

14 August 1725

JEAN BAPTISTE RAPHAEL—Free Negro, native of Martinique, son of Jean Raphael and Marguerite de St. Christophe, habitant of Martinique and MARIE GASPART—daughter of Jean Gaspart, drummer for the company of Le Blanc, and Agnes Simon, native of Bruger [or Bruges] in Flanders. [Married with the permission of Mr. Boisbriant, commandant general of this colony.]

5 April 1723

FRANCOIS RAYMOND called Bourgogne—native of Paris and JULIENNE NALIARD—native of Ennebon.

85

9 February 1732

LAMBERT REIBAUT called La Jeunesse—corporal in the company of Mr. de Pradel, native of La Cotte (?) St. Paul in Provence, bishopric of Vans, son of Etienne Reibaut and Francoise Reigaut and **LOUISE MARCHAND**—native of D'Erdon, bishopric of Vannes, daughter of Guillaume Marchand and Nicolle DesRoche, widow of Pierre Billiet called La Jeunesse, who died at Natchez.

26 June 1730

JEAN BAPTISTE REJAS called La Prade—resident on the lower Mississippi River, native of Quebec, son of Jean Baptiste Rejas and Marie Magdelaine Cloutier, widower of Elizabeth Faveau, who died at Paskagoulas and **ANGELIQUE GIRARDY**—daughter of Joseph Girardy and Francoise, an Indian, widow of Alain Duguet, who died at Natchez.

16 May 1730

CLAUDE RENAULT called Avignon—sergeant in the D'Artaguette Company, native of Avignon, son of Pierre Renault and Toinette Durand and **MARIE ANNE GRANDRY**—native of Metz, daughter of Jean Grandry and Barbe Lamy, widow of Antoine Alard called Postillon, who died at Natchez.

18 March 1721

CHARLES REQUIEM—son of Jean Requiem and Marie Cailla and **ANTOINETTE EULIE**—daughter of Pierre Eulie and Charlotte [Blank].

19 November 1720
On board the ship *Alexandre* at Old Fort Biloxi

CHARLES REQUIEM—native of the parish and town of Poitou and **MARIE MAGDELAINE ROSE**—native of the parish of Soyer.

25 June 1731

JEAN REVEL—native of Lisac, bishopric of Cahors, son of Marc Antoine Revel and Marie Pintie and HELEINE PALFERNE—native of Havre, daughter of Robert Palferne and Cecille Anselme, widow of Mathieu Braquiny, who died at the Old Fort.

19 April 1723

CHRISTIANNE RICHARD—native of Palatina and MARGUERITE ARENS—native of Hambourg.

19 April 1721

PIERRE RICHAUME—son of Jacques Richaume and Marguerite Graho and JEANNE FRANCOISE MAROYE—daughter of Pierre Francois Maroye and Marie Anne le Grand.

14 August 1721

JEAN RICHE—son of Jean Baptiste Richer and Perinne Anno and MARGUERITE GLODERERIOR—daughter of Felix Gloderio and Hubert Guillaume.

27 November 1730

LAURENT RIFFAU—inspector of the troops for the Company of the Indies, native of Belisle en Mer, diocese of Vannes, son of deceased Antonio Riffau, contractor for the King, and Marie Mordel and ANNE FOUILLETTE—native of Beaugé in Anjou, daughter of deceased René Fouillette, merchant, and Marie Galet.

20 February 1730

FRANCOIS ANTOINE RIVARD—son of deceased Antoine Rivard, resident of Ruisseaux St. Jean [Bayou St. Jean], and Marie Briard, native of the parish of Natchez, presently of this parish and JEANNE ANTOINETTE DE VUILLEMONT—daughter of deceased Henry Martin Moribois, Esquire, Sieur de Vuillemont, a concessioner of this colony while living, and Antoinette Fourier. "His wife" is widow in second marriage of deceased Rivard, also of this parish.

21 March 1729

ANTOINE RIVIERE—voyager, son of Jean Baptiste Riviere and Marie Barbe Champeau, native of St. Siphorin, bishopric of Chartres in Bosse and ETIENETTE AUFRET—daughter of Joseph Aufret and Marie Poulin.

3 June 1721

JACQUES ROBA—son of Blaise Roba and Marguerite Bourgerar and MARIE BARBE LE COMTE—daughter of Francois Le Comte and Marie Le Lou. [Then follows the following, seemingly garbled: *"ses pere et mere. de Mathieu Avignon fils de Michel Avignon et de Marthe _____ ses pere et mere et de Jeane Chevet fille de Jacques Chevet et de Marie Grepine ses pere et mere . . . . . Dalexandre Nicolas Capel fils de Gilbert Nicolas Capel de Petronille Lemoine ses pere et mere et de Perette Valiere, fille de Nicolas Vallie et de Genevieve de Belle Com- - - -. de Norbert de Villeneuve, fils de Jean Francois de Villeneuve et de Clair Charlemagne, ses pere et mere, et de Marie Jeanne Francois, fille de Guillaum Francois et Marie Louise Genel, ses pere et mere."*]

27 June 1721

ZACHARIE ROBAR—son of Jean Rorbar and Rose Guerin and ANGELIQUE GIRARD—daughter of André Girard and Charlotte Gatio.

2 February 1723

FRANCOIS ROBERGE—native of Paris, son of Denis Roberge and Jeanne Gibout of Paris and **MARIE BALLIS**—daughter of Francois le Ballis and Francois [Blank] .

27 August 1726

BONNAVENTURE ROBERT—master tailor, son of Nicolas Robert, master house-builder, and Marie Maique, native of the parish of Xaintes, bishopric of Vannes (?) and **MARIE PERON** (?)—daughter of Julien Pernon (?), and Louise Mareque, native of the parish of Landeau, bishopric of Vannes.

9 May 1726

JEAN ROBERT—native of Xaintonge, parish of Charante, son of Jean Robert and Marie Jeanne Gabrielle and **MARIE ROZE LE MOINE**—daughter of Nicolas Le Moine and Marie, an Indian.

15 May 1721

LOUIS ROBILLARD—son of Charles Robillard and Marie Ougeunarde and **MARIE MAGDELAINE CORDIER**—daughter of Louis Cordier and Magdelaine Marreine.

28 July 1732

JEAN ROBLAN—native of Rennes in Brittany, son of Jacques Roblan and Jacquette Amis and **VINCENTE CORLEE**—native of [?? lendgny], bishopric of Vannes, widow of Toussaint Boursilly, who died in Louisiana. The groom signed: Jan Roblot.

THE NEW ORLEANS FRENCH

20 October 1721

JEAN JACQUES ROCHORT and **LOUISE BOSNE** [or Bomme ?].

14 May 1731

PHILIPPE RODAIS called Calais—soldier of the company of Monsieur D'Artaguet, native of Lions, parish of St. Liziers, son of Etienne Rodais, silk-merchant, and Claudine Le Noir and **GUILLEMETTE LE ROUX**—native of the bourg of Languidy, bishopric of Vannes in Basse Bretagne, daughter of Cona Le Roux, *menuisier*, and Francoise Le Guian. In attendance was Marie Jeanne, age thirteen months, baptized at L'Orient, at the Church of St. Louis, of whom Philippe Calet recognized being the father.

5 April 1721

MATHURIN ROGER—son of Pierre Roger and Jeanne Hervane (?) and **CATHERINE BLANCHARD**—daughter of Pierre Blanchard. The mother is not given.

19 March 1728

FRANCOIS ROLLETT—native of St. Vincent, bishopric of Lucon, son of deceased Pierre Rollet and Marie Fromette and **FRANCOIS MANSARD**—native of Verdun, daughter of Nicolas Mansard and Marguerite Botson.

13 October 1727

JACQUES ROQUIGNY—Director of the Concession of Chouachas for Mr. Le Blanc, native of Dieppe, diocese of Rouan, son of deceased Jacques Roquigny, bourgeois of Rouan, and Marie Marguerite Bignon and **MARIE JOLY**—native of Paris, parish of St. Sulpice, daughter of deceased Louis Joly, bourgeois of Paris, and Marie Magdelaine Bessen.

THE NEW ORLEANS FRENCH

9 September 1720

JEAN ROSET [or Rozet] —soldier, native of Lauzanne in Switzerland, canton of Berne, son of Jean Jacques Roset and Marie Maurel and **MARGUERITE SALOS**—native of La Ferté sur Joy, diocese of Mau in Brie, daughter of Nicolas Salos and Anne Susanne.

27 November 1730

MICHEL ROSSARD—royal notary and secretary-in-chief for the province of Louisiana, native of the town of Blois, widower of Marguerite Gilberte de la Gardette, who died at Paris and **LOUISE DE MARGANNE DE LA VALTERIE**—daughter of deceased Seraphim de Marganne, esquire, Seigneur de la Valterie, and Louise Bissot de la Valterie, widow of Monsieur Dutisné, captain of the detached company of the Marine, commandant at Illinois.

7 August 1721

PHILIPPE ROUET—son of Pierre Rouet and Suzanne Delisle and **ANNE DUMENY**—widow of Jean Pirogue, daughter of Samuel Demier (?) and Marie Leonard.

12 April 1730

FRANCOIS ROUGEAU—native of Hyrancy, diocese of Auxerre, son of Pierre Rougeau and Aimée Chapotin and **ANGELIQUE CHARTRON**—native of Dain [should be Hedin] in Artois, bishopric of St. Omer, daughter of Adrien Chartron and Marie Anne Vasseur, widow of Laurent Denoyers, major of the post of Natchez, while living.

THE NEW ORLEANS FRENCH

16 April 1730

NICOLAS ROUSSAUD—resident of Natchez, son of Nicolas Roussaud and Genevieve Du Chemin, native of Montreau, bishopric of Sens in Bourgogne, widower of Anne Degravelle, who died in Louisiana and CATHERINE DUCOSSE—native of Bayonne, daughter of Jean Ducosse called Nota and Catherine Trouillet. [Ed. note—Where Ducosse appears, Notache was scratched through and Ducrosse written above in the same hand.] She was the widow of Laurent Hurlatte, who died at Natchez.

16 April 1730

LOUIS ROY—native of Montreal, parish of St. Lambert, son of Pierre Roy and Marie Catherine Ducharme, widower of Marguerite Dumay, who died in Louisiana and MARIE JEANNE MAGNUS—daughter of Charles Magnus and Marie Catherine Boblée, native of Chaumont, bishopric of Cambray, widow of Reinne, who died at Natchez.

22 March 1721

RENE SABOURIN—son of René Sabourin and Catherine Delizier (?) and MARIE CATHERINE FOUCAULT—daughter of Jean Baptiste Foucault and Marie Francoise Nicole Defer.

18 April 1730

JACQUES SANTIER—son of Joseph Santier and Dominique Franchet, native of Seicelle (?) in Bugay (?), bishopric of Bellay and MARIE L'EPRON—daughter of Simon L'Epron and Suzanne Rebourd, native of Drolan, bishopric of Caux, widow of Pierre Bernard, who died in Louisiana.

THE NEW ORLEANS FRENCH

23 April 1721

PIERRE SANTORIN—son of Antoine Santorin and Marie Francoise and **GENEVIEVE BILLARD**—daughter of Pierre Billard and Jeanne Cadet.

1 March 1726

JACQUES SAUNIE—heretofore soldier in the Company of D'Artus, captain in the regiment of the Marie, resident of New Orleans, makes abjuration of the heresy of Calvinism in which he was born and reared.

17 April 1730

FRANCOIS SAUNIER—master wet-cooper of Paris, son of Augustin Saunier, also a master wet-cooper at Paris and Louise De Val, native of the parish of St. Germain de Lauxeroy, bishopric of Paris and **MAGDE-LAINE NEIRE**—daughter of André Neire and Anne Vebre, native of the parish of the town of Vallin in Switzerland.

8 July 1721

BARTHELEMY SEANCE—son of Pierre Seance and Marie Catherine Renas and **MARIE JACQUELINE DUBOS**—daughter of René Dubos and Elizabeth Claire Valons.

30 January 1730

FRANCOIS SEIMARD DE BELISLE—officer in the troops of this colony, son of Francois Seimard, mayor of Fontenay in Poitou, and Dame Anne Monet Fleury, native of Fontenay, parish of Notre Dame and **MARGUERITE ENOULT DE LIVAUDAIS**—native of St. Malo, daughter of deceased Jacques Enoult de Livaudais and Dame Marie Le Jaloux.

THE NEW ORLEANS FRENCH

6 February 1731

JEAN SERGENT called Dubuisson—resident (?) of Boulogne, son of Jean Sergent and Marie Anne Prevot, widower of Marie Dubois, who died in Louisiana and **PERINNE GROSSIN**—native of St. Siruan, bishopric of St. Malo, daughter of Francois Grossin and Marie Boquet.

26 December 1726

MICHEL SERING—widower of Ursule Specte, who died in Louisiana and **BARBE HERTLE**—widow of Joseph Bailly, who died in Louisiana.

14 July 1725

MATHURIN SIMARD—native of La Tremblade, diocese of Xaintonge, son of Vincent Simard and Anne Bricou, sailor for the Company and **ANNE VIGNODE**—native of La Tremblade, daughter of deceased Andre Vignode and Anne Magnier.

13 June 1723, Fort Louis called The Biloxi

JOSEPH SIMON, Sieur de la Pointe—widower and habitant and **CATHERINE DOUCIN**—widow. Note: Lapointe has a little girl about two years old.

10 July 1723

JACQUES FRANCOIS SIMPEL—native of the parish of La Gorgne in Flanders, son of Jacques Simpel and Suzanne Roussel, being sick in bed, but sound in mind, says that on 24 February 1721, he contracted marriage with **JEANNE FORT**—daughter of Pierre Fort and Marie Guicon, native of Gray in Comté. But, vows the groom, for reasons known to himself, he substituted "Paul Le Bleu" for his real name given above. The couple renews vows.

THE NEW ORLEANS FRENCH

1 July 1720

PIERRE SINTON–native of Chatellereau, son of Maitre Adrien Sinton and Francoise Reffay and **NICOLE DUVENNE (?)**–native of Chalon in Chapagne, daughter of Philipe Duvenne and Anne Caff.

15 July 1721

ANTOINE SOREL–son of Michel Sorel and Marguerite Second and **ANNE ROLAIS**–daughter of Martin Rolais and Perine Lafleur.

3 February 1722

ALEXANDRE NORBERT SPEEQUE–native of the town of Furne, parish of St. Nicolas and **MARIE BARBE DUMAN**. Both are workers for the Royal Company of the Indies at Fort Louis.

26 August 1720

CHARLES ST. PRIX–native of Tour in Tourraine, son of Charles St. Prix and Marie Collin and **LIRIINE (?) FRANCOISE GUILLOT**–native of Paris, daughter of Simon Guillot and Agathe Martin.

29 July 1720

PIERRE TEXIER–son of deceased Pierre Texier, while living, of La Rochelle, parish of St. Augustin, bishopric of Xaintes in Saintonge, and Francois Guinare and **MARIE JEANNE GOGUET**–native of Arras in Artois, daughter of Jean Goguet and Marie du Fablon.

95

THE NEW ORLEANS FRENCH

24 February 1721, Biloxi

PIERRE TEXIER—son of Glaude Texier and Louise Pilon and **MARIE ANNE JOURNE**—daughter of Guillaume Journé and Louise Genevieve.

10 August 1732

THEODORE and **MARIE CLAUDE**, Negro slaves belonging to De Noyant.

15 February 1723, German Coast

GASPART THILLY—son of Jacques Thilly and Barbe Osvaldy (?), bourgeois in Alsace and **ELIZABETH STOZLE**—native of Alsace.

16 May 1730

CHRISTOPH THOMAS—native of Condé, bishopric of Toual, son of Nicolas Thomas and Marguerite Leseure and **MARIE ANNE ROUSSEAU**—native of St. Jean d'Angelique, bishopric of Sainte, widow of Pierre Lartaud, who died at Natchez.

19 March 1727

PIERRE THOMMELIN—native of Dunkerque, widower of Marguerite Cussonnette who died at Dunkerque and **GENIVIEVE CARON**—native of Paris, widow of Jean Louis de Lestre.

23 February 1722, Natchez

FRANCOIS THORET—son of Jean Thoret and Jacqueline Legrand and **ENE** (?) [Probably: Eve] **DURIE**—daughter of Joseph Durie and Elizabeth Troe.

96

THE NEW ORLEANS FRENCH

1 July 1721

FRANCOIS TOUCHE—son of René Touché and Jeanne Lemarie and **JOSEPH LE NOBLE**—daughter of Francois Le Noble and Marie Jeanne Sebastien.

9 March 1723

FRANCOIS TOURETTE—surgeon-soldier of Richebourg's Company and **OLIVE LAHAINS**—native of L'Orient, widow of Raymond Baldiere.

1 July 1727, Yazoo Post

HENRY TOURTEBAT—native of Charbonne, archbishopric of Rheims, resident of New Orleans and **TOINETTE JEANLOTTE**—native of Barbeduc [or Barleduc] in Lorraine. This is a certification made on 9 July 1730. The original, signed by Pere Suel, Jesuit, acting priest at the Yazoo Post, was burned by the Indians.

7 November 1731

JOSEPH TURPIN—native of Montreal, son of deceased Alexandre Turpin and deceased Charlotte Beauvais, of the parish of Kaskaskias and **HYPPOLITTE**—daughter of an Indian named Catherine, once a servant of Chauvin de la Freniere.

19 April 1723

CLAUDE VACHON—son of Louis Vachon native of [Blank] in Auvergne and **MARIE DAMILION**—daughter of Mathieu Damilion and Louise Le Vieux, native of Strasbourg.

97

10 February 1721

JACQUES VALADE—son of Mathurin Valade and Elizabeth Dolette, native of La Rochelle and MARTHE BUNELLE [or Burelle].

5 May 1721

JEAN VANEUL—son of André Vaneul and Jeanne Roun and ANDRI-ANNE HAREY—daughter of André Harey and Jaquet Vanderal.

19 March 1731

SIMON VANON—Free Negro, native of Senegal and MARIE AMO—Free Negro, native of Senegal. [Ed. note—The groom signed in a clear and firm hand: Simon Vanon.]

25 June 1726

ALEXANDRE BERNARD VIELLE—surgeon-major of New Orleans, son of Pierre Vielle, bourgeois of Paris, and Elizabeth Le Blanc, native of the parish of St. Nicolas des Champs and SERUANNE PERINNE LAURENCE LE BLANC—daughter of deceased Henry Le Blanc, guardian of the storehouse, and Seruanne Lemarié.

28 April 1727

MICHEL VIEN—son of deceased Jean Baptiste Vien and Catherine Gatteau of the parish of Champlain, bishopric of Quebec in Canada and MARIE FRANCOISE LE VERT—daughter of deceased Jacques le Vert and Jeanne Cochois, who died here, native of the parish of St. Nicolas des Champ, Paris and *belle-fille* of Jacob, who is employed by the Company.

THE NEW ORLEANS FRENCH

13 March 1722, probably at Natchez

LOUIS VIGER—son of Denis Viger and Catherine Motier and MARIE
ANNE GIRODON—daughter of Pierre Girodon and Dovame [or Dor-
ame] [possibly Dovanne, etc.]

29 May 1722

JEAN VILER—son of André Viler and Anne de Romure, native of the
parish of St. Paul in Lyon and ANNE BARBE MAYER—daughter of
Adam Mayer and Dorothée [Blank].

14 August 1721

CHARLES VINCENT—son of Francois Vincent and Marie Samson and
MARIE MARGUERITE LE JEUNE—daughter of Claude Le Jeune and
Marie Anne Le Sueur.

6 February 1731

NICOLAS VISE—son of Jean Vise and Marguerite Buteler, native of
Wolkringen, canton of Berne and MARTE MAGDELAINE BINTON—
daughter of Jean Adam Binten and Marie Catherine, native of Arenbach,
widow of Jean Setuky (?), who died at Natchez.

10 June 1721

GUILLAUME VIVIER—son of Jean Vivier and Marie [Blank] Moreau
and MAGDELAINE VILLEROY—daughter of Jean Villeroy and Francoise [Blank].

99

2 February 1728

JEAN WECHEN [or Wechers] —native of Gautoome (?) [Gasstonne ?] ,
bishopric of Strasbourg, son of Jean Michel Weche - - - (?) and Magdelaine Buhler, in a third marriage of Marie Studelee, who died at Cannes
Bruslées and MARIE MAGDELAINE AKERMAN—daughter of Michel
Akerman and Marie Anne Abvenden.

3 June 1729

JACQUES WEISKREMER—native of Bavaria, son of deceased Abraham
Weiskremer and Magdelaine Nedemarin, widower of Anne Marguerite
Beierin (?), who died at the Fort de la Balize and EMERENTIANE
LOTTERMAN—native of the Canton of Berne, Switzerland, widow of
Maurice Kobler, who died in Louisiana.

30 July 1731

FRANCOIS ZAPIAU—native of Montarmagnie, bishopric of Langres,
son of Francois Zapiau and Nicolle Durau and ELIZABETH VUITRI-
QUIN—daughter of Francois Vuitriquin and Charlotte Hegue, native of
Maubuche.

ADDENDA

22 March 1723

PENCRASSE AUBERMOND—native of Suril, soldier in Baumont's Company and **MARIE HANSEIN**—native of Alsace.

5 April 1728

JACQUES HUBERT BELAIRE—native of Montreal, son of deceased Ignace Hubert and Barbe Chauvin, and **MARGUERITE CATHERINE NEVEU**—native of Montreal, daughter of deceased Jacques Neveu and Michel Chauvin, widow of Etienne Roy, who died in Louisiana. The parties are of second degree consanguinity.

THE PRIESTS

The following list is a compilation of officiating and assisting priests as reflected in the records contained in this book. Sister Gertrude's name appeared in only one record.

1720 - Prothay [at New Biloxi]
1721 - Sister Gertrude
1721-1723 - Richard
1721 - Duval
1721 - Rossard
1721 - Joseph de St. Charles
1721 - Le Moriniere
1721 - Charles Carme de Chaussez
1721-1722 - Darquevaux
1722-1723 - Dorez
1722 - Maximum [of Natchez]
1722-1723 - Bruno de Langre
1723 - - Eusebe de Chaumont
1723 - Philibert
1723-1732 - Raphael de Luxembourg
1723-1725 - Christophe de Chaumont
1724 - Caston [Aumonier of *Le Profond*)
1725 - Mathias de Sedan
1725-1733 - Hyacinthe de Verdun
1727-1728 - Theodore
1728, 1730, 1731 - Philippe de Luxembourg
1730-1733 - Pierre
1730 - Fleurian
1731 - Barthelemy Gauchet

INDEX

105

INDEX

COULONGE, 79
COURLIE, 16
COUSSENOTE, 61
COUTURIER, 21
CRANNE, 7
CRESPEL, 11
CRETHE, 70
CRETZ, 7
CREUNE, 70
CRIE, 54
CROUSTELHAS, 37
CROUSTILHAD, 67
CUICHET, 52
CULIOT, 21
CURE, 40
CUSSON, 4
CUSSONNETTE, 96

D'ERIE, 3
D'ESPANNET, 28
D'ESPERON, 30
D'ESTENDRE, 61
D'ILLERIN, 32
D'OSTENDE, 71
DAMAS, 65
DAMASEAU, 13
DAMILION, 97
DAMMOURETTE, 77
DAN, 10
DANFENTEO, 50
DANIEL, 10, 25, 54
DANUE, 49
DARBY, 73
DARTI, 26
DAUAUDE, 31
DAUBLIN, 22
DAUDESSO, 12
DAUDIN, 59
DAUPHIN, 8, 27, 28
DAUTRICOURT, 26
DAUVERGNE, 22
DE BASCHEMIN, 84
DE BEAUVAIS, 52
DE BELISLE, 93
DE BELLE COM.., 88
DE BERNON, 19
DE BIENVILLE, 52, 53, 54
DE BREBOEUF, 63
DE BREZ, 48
DE CHANAU, 13
DE FONTAINE, 33

DE FOSSE, 34
DE FRANCE, 15
DE GALLAIS, 63
DE HAYE, 19
DE L'ESTRIER, 29
DE L'ETANG, 3
DE LA BOULAY, 48, 66
DE LA BOULEE, 29
DE LA CHAISE, 29, 82, 83
DE LA COSTE, 12
DE LA GARDE, 31
DE LA HAUTE MAISON, 47
DE LA HAYE, 74
DE LA JOYE, 30
DE LA MASSONNE, 31
DE LA POINTE, 94
DE LA POMMERAY, 66
DE LA ROUSSELIERE, 32
DE LA TOUR, 68
DE LA VALTERIE, 91
DE LA VERENDRIE, 79
DE LAMARE, 17
DE LAMAZE, 82
DE LAUNAY, 7
DE LESTRE, 96
DE LIBERAT, 24
DE LIEGE, 73
DE LIVAUDAIS, 93
DE LIVILLIER, 79
DE LORDRE, 14
DE LORMEAU, 31
DE MALEDAN, 82
DE MANDEVILLE, 17
DE MARGANNE, 91
DE MERGERY, 31
DE NEUVILLE, 63
DE NOYANT, 96
DE PAIN, 7
DE PERRIER, 29
DE RENNE, 18
DE RIANT, 32
DE ROCHECHOUART, 13
DE ROMURE, 99
DE ST. CHRISTOPHE, 85

DE SENDISVILLE, 47
DE VAL, 93
DE VAUBERY, 52
DE VERRASAC, 33
DE VERTEUIL, 79
DE VILLENEUVE, 88
DE VUILLEMONT, 88
DEBROSSE, 29
DECOUBLANT, 33
DECUIR, 26
DEFER, 39, 92
DEGRAVELLE, 92
DELARMAS, 28
DELAUNAY, 34
DELETEE, 67
DELFONE, 34
DELISLE, 91
DELIZIER, 92
DELONAY, 53, 59
DELOUNAY, 58
DELSINE, 15
DELURY, 33
DEMARET, 75
DEMERON, 71
DEMIER, 91
DEMONS, 59
DENIS, 80
DENOYERS, 91
DEPASSE, 7
DERBO, 32
DERESON, 31
DERMUZEAU, 66
DERO, 42
DEROZE, 32
DES MILETS, 52
DESCORMIER, 22
DESCROS, 37
DESHAYE, 4
DESHAYES, 19
DESLESME, 64
DESMONTS, 21
DESMUZEAU, 66
DESPIE, 33
DESROCHE, 86
DIDIER, 71
DIMANCHE, 10
DINAN, 19
DINIER, 58
DIRAN, 16
DOLETTE, 98

107

INDEX

PERRAULT, 60
PERRIER, 85
PERROT, 62
PERSONET, 12
PERTHUIS, 10
PERUSSY, 26
PETIT, 29
PEVIFUE, 6
PEZIER, 18
PHILBERT, 22, 78
PHILIPPEAUX, 73
PICARD, 6
PICOU, 45
PIDTON, 50
PIE, 81
PIEL, 66
PIERON, 14
PIERRE, 29
PIERREMOND, 37
PIGNON, 58
PILON, 96
PIN, 73
PINARD, 20
PINAU, 41
PINTIE, 87
PIPE, 32
PLONZARD, 9
POINIER, 28
POIRIER, 53
POITEVINE, 24
POITTEVINE, 9
POLERY, 22
POLETTE, 38
POMMIER, 28
POMON, 81
PONSON, 81
POSAN, 43
POSTILLON, 86
POTEVIN, 47
POTIN, 9
POTVIN, 32
POUILLOT, 21
POULAIN, 80
POULIN, 88
POUPON, 83
POUPPON, 80
POUSSET, 65
POUSSIN, 59
PRADEAU, 30
PRAT, 29
PREVOST, 47
PREVOT, 94
PREZ, 80, 82

PRIPONET, 13
PRO, 55
PROUETTE, 10
PUILLONT, 57

QUARANTAY, 24
QUINDREMAN, 74

RABOUIN, 44
RABU, 40
RACLOT, 16
RAFLON, 50
RAZARD, 78
REBOURD, 92
REFFAY, 95
REHEBIN, 25
REIGAUT, 86
REINNE, 92
REITRE, 49
RENARD, 27, 60, 72
RENAS, 93
RENAUD, 47, 76
RENAUDOT, 64
RESALT, 30
RIAUT, 28
RICAR, 57
RICHARD, 16, 40, 45
RICHARDE, 45
RICHAUME, 10
RICHER, 22
RIDEN, 55
RIDER, 55
RISTER, 23
RITCHAY, 51
RITTER, 45
RIVARD, 88
RIVART, 14, 57
RIXENER, 55
ROAN, 60
ROBERT, 76
ROBLOT, 89
ROCH, 4
ROCHECHUART, 13
ROCHELLE, 17
RODE, 8
RODEN, 55
ROGER, 22, 35
ROLAIS, 95
ROLAND, 13
ROMMEL, 25
RONDEAU, 21
RONDELLE, 62
RONDOT, 15

RONNADE, 45
RORNIE, 83
ROSE, 69, 86
ROSSARD, 37, 61
ROSSERT, 29
ROUAN, 47
ROUAU, 47
ROUET, 16
ROUN, 98
ROUSSAU, 29
ROUSSAUD, 14, 47
ROUSSEAU, 56, 60, 96
ROUSSEL, 94
ROUSSET, 83
ROUSSIN, 38
ROY, 3, 30, 33, 51, 60, 103
ROZET, 91
RUELAN, 56, 77
RUFRAN, 70
RUFRAY, 70
RUICAM, 62

SACEQUEPEE, 80
ST. ANNE, 48
ST. ANTOINE, 23
ST. AUBIN, 53
ST. CAUTIN, 9
ST. GERMAIN, 49
ST. JACQUES, 8
ST. JEAN PATRON, 17
ST. LAURENT, 49
ST. LOUIS, 68
SALAHUN, 9
SALAIN, 5
SALMON, 31
SALONE, 44
SALOS, 91
SAMSON, 99
SAMURAN, 5
SANS CHAGRIN, 64
SANS LOUIS, 68
SARAZIN, 38
SARE, 85
SARRAZIN, 13
SATTEL, 83
SAUMERINE, 63
SAUSSE, 25
SAVARIE, 46
SAVARY, 20, 68
SCHANTZ, 76
SCHAT, 47

INDEX